A Partnership of
Similar Hearts

A Collaborative Approach to Deacon/Pastor Ministry at St. James Baptist Church

DR. JEROME LEE, JR.

authorHOUSE®

A PARTNERSHIP OF SIMILAR HEARTS:
A COLLABORATIVE APPROACH TO DEACON/PASTOR MINISTRY AT
ST. JAMES BAPTIST CHURCH

A Doctor of Ministry Project
Submitted to the Faculty of the
School of Theology

of

VIRGINIA UNION UNIVERSITY

in partial fulfillment of
the requirements for the degree of

DOCTOR OF MINISTRY

by

Jerome Lee, Jr.

Richmond, Virginia
May 2015

AuthorHouse™
1663 Liberty Drive
Bloomington, IN 47403
www.authorhouse.com
Phone: 1 (800) 839-8640

Published by AuthorHouse 11/18/2016

ISBN: 978-1-5246-5055-1 (sc)
ISBN: 978-1-5246-5054-4 (e)

Samuel DeWitt Proctor School of Theology
Virginia Union University

This is to certify that the Project Documentation by Jerome Lee Jr. entitled, "A Partnership of Similar Hearts: A Collaborative Approach to Deacon/Pastor Ministry at St. James Baptist Church", has been approved by this committee as satisfactory completion of the Program requirement for the degree of Doctor of Ministry.

_____

Program Director and School Name

_____

Advisor/Committee Member

_____

Dean of School

_____

Date

ABSTRACT

"A Partnership of Similar Hearts: A Collaborative Approach to Deacon/Pastor Ministry at St. James Baptist Church"

By Jerome Lee, Jr., M.Div., Virginia Union University

A Project Document submitted in partial fulfillment of the requirements for the degree of Doctor of Ministry, at Virginia Union University

Virginia Union University, 2015

Dr. Patricia Gould-Champ, Assistant Professor of Practical Theology, School of Theology

This applied ministerial project, "A Partnership of Similar Hearts: A Collaborative Approach to Deacon/Pastor Ministry at St. James Baptist Church" examined the knowledge base of the current deacon ministry and its correlation to effective ministry in serving the needs of the St. James Baptist Church (SJBC) family in Greensboro, NC. Coupled with this examination was the need for collaboration between the pastor and deacons in so doing. This project was designed to infuse the integration of the belief systems of the current deacon ministry with training that better serves the people and causes better collaboration with the pastor. This project did address the social problems that the overall deacon ministry of SJBC could face while serving. To add, this project also ensures all aspects of ministry were reflective of the paradigm shift that had taken place within the church, particularly in the area of leadership training. Demands placed by diverse parishioners on the urban pastor and the deacons seem to require the pastor less hands on, while relegating many of the essential duties to servant leadership.

These demands necessitated a partnership of similar hearts and a collaborative approach to ministry.

Through the use of surveys, questionnaires, interviews, focus groups and continual training, information gleaned was used to develop a training model for the deacons. In "A Partnership of Similar Hearts: A Collaborative Approach to Deacon/Pastor Ministry at St. James Baptist Church", relevant cutting edge deacon training was essential. Training for the deacons served as the conduit for the collaborative transformation of similar hearts to occur.

DEDICATION

The work of the project is dedicated to the many persons that have influenced my life. To my parents, Jerome Lee, Sr. and Sandra Y. Packett, who nurtured me with love and discipline. To my Grandma, Marie H. Cox, for making me pray in the days of my youth even when I didn't want to pray. She was loving, giving and full of humor. Her voice has now been silenced by death (I miss you). To my beautiful wife, Cynthia, with whom I celebrate 23 years of marriage, I am so blessed. Thank you for your willingness to assist me in every endeavor that I have taken on this spiritual journey. Your strength is incredible. And too the Africans, the most precious cargo that has every crossed the Atlantic Ocean, of whom I am a descendent until I perish. To God Be Glory!

ACKNOWLEDGEMENTS

The fact that this ministry project has come to a full, required completion, represents the culmination of an assiduous work that has an intentional effort to bless the St. James Baptist Church (SJBC) family and those churches that may benefit from its use. Although I cannot mention everyone, I cannot begin to acknowledge anyone without first acknowledging my eternal Savior and Lord, Jesus Christ. He is the inspiration that motivates me to do a greater work for His kingdom. I am grateful and extend my sincere gratitude to the School of Theology at Virginia Union University (STVU), for being the tool in challenging and shaping my own theological acuity.

The Master of Divinity and Doctor of Ministry studies has been beneficial to my ministry assignment as pastor, because of the intellectually stimulating resources, carefully constructed critiques and thought-provoking, yet extensive suggestions provided by the staff of STVU. They are so dedicated to the field of theology, that they found it not robbery to write and publish books of help themselves. Thanks to Dr. Gloria Taylor who is currently retired from teaching at STVU. She served as my instructor in Christian Education and also as my advisor, in the early foundation of this work in progress. An enormous appreciation goes to Dr. Patricia Gould-Champ for extending her hand and committing herself to the final work of this project. You could have said no, but you did not.

The time and effort it takes to do research, collect data and other necessary resources that will contribute to this project, became a collaborative effort for myself and those persons who obligated themselves to assist me in this spiritual journey. They were able to help create an atmosphere of working relationships and transformation between pastor and diaconate. Their support has made the difference in me doing my best in producing a quality work.

I owe a special word of thanks to the St. James Baptist Church for being a congregation that is an advocate of education and allowing me the privilege of pursuing my heart in what will be a benefit for all. I would be remiss if I did not express my gratitude to the deacons and deaconesses, both of SJBC for participating in the trainings, workshops, conferences and questionnaires that continue to give me the wisdom, insight and foresight to create a strong diaconate that will be an asset for the 21st century church.

I am very appreciative for the support of my spiritual father, pastor and mentor, the Rev. Dr. Dwight Riddick, Sr. of the Gethsemane Baptist Church, Newport News, VA. Pastor Riddick is currently the president of the Hampton University Ministry Conference (2015-2018). I am forever in debt to my family for their support and prayers in all that I do. In particular, a great thank you to my parents, Jerome Lee Sr. and Sandra Packett for giving birth to me and instilling in me the ethic of persistence. Thank you! Finally to my wife, Cynthia, a virtuous and praying woman, who has so beautifully believed in me and who has forsaken all to allow God to be glorified in her. "Can two walk together except they agree?" (Amos 3:3, KJV).

TABLE OF CONTENTS

APPENDICES

ABBREVIATIONS

AIDS	Acquired Immunodeficiency Syndrome
EBC	Ebenezer Baptist Church
E.S.V.A	Eastern Shore of Virginia
HPEMBA	High Point Education and Missionary Baptist Association
KJV	King James Version
KWL	What you KNOW, What You WANT to know, What you LEARNED
NIV	New International Version
NKJV	New King James Version
OPC	Orthodox Presbyterian Church
OTJ	On the job training
SJBC	St. James Baptist Church
STVU	School of Theology Virginia Union

DEFINITIONS

church polity	The ministerial structure of a church and its authority relationships.
collaborative approach	The style of working together as in a joint intellectual effort.
conflict resolution	The process of resolving a dispute or a conflict by meeting at least some of each side's needs.
diaconate	The office or period of office of a deacon (male and female).
edifice complex	When leadership focuses on the physical structure versus the spiritual structure.

paradigm shift   A change in the basic assumption within the ruling theory of science, according to Thomas Kuhn; change of one way of thinking with another.

pedagogical approach   Of or related to teachers training or education.

re-envisioning   The process of thinking of something that one believes might exist or happen in the future.

servant leadership   The idea of one serving the people that he/she leads.

team building   The use of different types of group interventions for enhancing social relations and clarifying members' roles.

urban   Of, relating to, or location in a city.

INTRODUCTION

Reader's Expectations

A collaborative approach to deacon/pastor ministry at Saint James Baptist Church (SJBC) requires a partnership of similar hearts through training. As a result of experiential learning and fifteen years of pastoral training in both rural and urban contexts, the researcher found that both settings are not only similar but necessary. Their similarities in deacon training can be described as steeped in tradition yet lacking structured training. The reader can expect to receive guidance on how to develop a process which transforms deacon training and embraces a partnership of similar hearts. Furthermore, the reader can expect an analysis of the training and development of deacon ministry at SJBC with recommendations for its continued growth and collaboration.

Problem Statement

There is a need to define the roles and responsibilities of the deacon at SJBC in light of changing times. The church leadership, consisting primarily of pastor and deacons, may not be fully aware of the future change movement needed to properly serve the community. "Most churches in America are hampered by stifling traditions, outdated programs and lifeless institutional processes."[1] The current deacon leadership at SJBC epitomizes this contradiction. We must re-envision how we conduct church. We must re-envision the roles and responsibilities of the deacon. Moreover, we must re-envision how the deacon serves the pastor and people through a collaborative approach. Every aspect of ministry must be thoroughly examined and reshaped to meet the dynamic and changing needs at SJBC. Those needs included church healing, developing and maintaining a

---

[1] Kim Simmons and Mike Simmons, "Visions for 21st Century Ministry Design and Community Transformation," *PowerLife*, accessed March 3, 2015, http://w2ww.powerlife.org/Consulting/Vision.html#top.

positive relationship between the pastor and the deacon ministry. Additionally, there was a need to re-examine the role of the deaconess. Educating leadership, specifically the deacon ministry, has to be the first step in ministry transformation. Currently, the SJBC deacon ministry consists of deacons across a continuum of spiritual maturity, ages and different skill sets. Some are more experienced than others when it comes to performing duties of the deacon. Therefore, the challenge remains at the forefront for effective training and establishing a partnership with the pastor at SJBC.

Model for Ministry

The intention of this project is to prepare deacons to serve in the ministry. According to Kate Ward-Turner, "No deacon is suitably qualified to exercise the office of deacon until he is adequately trained for the office. Thus, to say that a deacon is qualified for an office is to say that he is sufficiently trained for the work of the deacon."[2] A curriculum was developed considering the gravity of the state of deacon development. Inclusive in this project was a full year of pastoral observation, preparation, followed by approximately two years of training and implementation. Deacons historically have received 'on the job training'. In the secular world, 'on the job training' (OJT) is provided to inexperienced employees during the initial stages of employment. This is usually provided by a professional trainer or experienced employee and typically consist of 'hands-on-training.'[3] We named them as deacons and released them without proper orientation of their roles and responsibilities. For many years this type of training has sufficed. The above practices are not necessarily realistic for today's church or its

---

[2] Kate Ward-Turner, *Deacon Training* (New York: iUniverse, Inc, 2008.), 41.

[3] "What is ON THE JOB TRAINING (OJT)?" *Black's Law Dictionary Online* 2nd ed., accessed March 10, 2014, www.thelawdictionary.org/OJT.

functions. However, in more recent years the need for more specialized Christian Education for the body has evolved. Unfortunately, effective training takes place everywhere but not in the church. This places a hardship on the relationship between pastors and deacons.

While the church has structure, it is sorely lacking in effective training strategies that catapult the thinking and understanding of leadership towards a collective partnership for training in ministry. Therefore, a pedagogical and collaborative approach to leadership transformation is critical. This project will attempt to educate deacon leadership by utilizing a planned framework of instruction conducive to improving the ministry itself. "While the whole church is obligated to make sure that deacons are trained for the deacon ministry, the responsibility rest primarily with the pastor. No undertaking by the pastor is more imperative."[4]

This curriculum model for ministry will realign the previously stated needs of SJBC. This model for ministry's focus will be to realign the deacon's current practices with both scripture and the needs of the church. The deacons have received minimal training during their tenure of service. However, the training has not been consistent, continual, nor has it been congruent in transforming skill sets beyond serving communion, visitations and counting monies. Although these areas are very important, they are limiting and superficial in scope compared to the depth of ministry needs. Very little emphasis has been placed on the pastor and deacon relationship. Our soldiers in the military must get beyond basic training to become effective leaders. This comes through continual education, training and re-training. This model will invoke a realization of deacon deficits and/or encourage the deacon into a more specialized and intensive service

---

[4] Ward-Turner, 35.

that includes the pastoral partnership. The deacon must serve honorably with knowledge and power or otherwise risk being a liability for kingdom living and building. Therefore, it is imperative that the curriculum model for ministry educates and re-educates the deacon ministry through a more in-depth and comprehensive study of genuine servant leadership.

Hypothesis and Insight

The hypothesis explored in this ministry model: training is conducted for the deacons in order that they may be effectively prepared to serve and minister to the body of Christ. There is a need for specific training and re-envisioning. When the researcher helps them to re-envision, they will be better equipped to do the job as a deacon and also develop a similar heart of the pastor. The researcher believes that training for the deacon has been limited because of the primary functions deacons performed historically. There is not much perceived training needed in serving communion, counting money, visitation or even maintaining a solid relationship with the pastor. With this limited viewpoint of what being a servant leader included, the expectations could remain low and of minimal effect. According to Marvin A. McMickle's citation of J. Newton Brown's work, *A Baptist Church Manual* first published in 1853:

> It seems to reinforce this understanding that the work of the deacon was not limited to spiritual matters, but also included some supervision of the temporal affairs of the church. It shall be the duty of the deacons to seek out such members of the church as need assistance, and to use the alms of the church for their relief; to visit the sick; to prepare and distribute the elements of the Lord's Supper; to take a general supervision of temporal interest of the church, and to cooperate with and assist the pastor in the performance of his duties.[5]

---

[5] Marvin A. McMickle, *Deacons in Today's Black Baptist Church* (Valley Forge, PA: Judson Press, 2010), 37.

Hence, the researcher concluded the need to re-envision the deacons as servant leaders reflecting change in a dynamically, diverse church setting and culture.

Overview

Educating, re-training and addressing servant leadership challenges can be all in a day's work if the deacon ministry wants to become strong and vibrant. However, due to the disconnection, a collaborative approach was not evident. When service has limited opportunity to be developed and transformed, ministry can become burdensome and even stalemate. It is the researcher's intention to lead the deacons into a stronger, more developed synthesis of Bible application and understanding of service. A deacon that knows how to mitigate the deficits through proper understanding and application of the scripture is one that will better serve the people over which they have charge. Their service can no longer be superficial. It must reflect the heart of Christ, the heart of the pastor and the needs of the people. However, there was a disconnection at SJBC.

The initial phase of this project is accomplished by setting its expectations. Emphasis is placed on articulating what the problem statement is in this model project and how it interfaces within and without its contextual framework. The researcher has spent the last four years as pastor of SJBC in Greensboro, North Carolina and found a profound disparity in the training norms, or lack thereof, in the deacon ministry. Due to several years without a pastor, the deacons led the ministry. Their priority was just to "keep things going." Training was not evident. Even before the church was without a pastor, training tended to be piecemeal. The deacon leaders did attend Sunday school and sometimes Bible Study. However, the opportunity to complete their servanthood in an official, organized capacity was limited or nonexistent. Their training was inadequate, not enough to address successfully the myriad of needs reflective in the ministry. The impetus for this project is to focus on reshaping the traditional mindset of the eighteen deacons at SJBC, while incorporating the training model and its emphasis on the deacon/pastor relationship. Following is an overview of the content found in each chapter.

Chapter I

The reader will find how the researcher's spiritual journey and personal transformation epitomizes servant leadership in his calling to the pastorate. The researcher spent exceptional time discovering who he is and the education inherent in his position as pastor. Training was always at the heart of the researcher's leadership. From his marked salvation experience, the researcher found himself at the feet of his mentor, always eager to learn as much of the Word as he could digest. As mentor, Dr. Dwight Riddick lovingly pushed and provoked the researcher to a standard of excellence as a learned and astute leader. Teaching and being taught was always paramount in how he performed the sacerdotal duties. It was not enough to just know the Word. The researcher also needed to know how to appropriately apply it.

Using his own personal experiences, the researcher used this as a backdrop for developing humility and a yearning for learning all about the Word. Without a planned program for growth, the researcher knew it would be highly impossible for him to grow in stature with those individuals who partnered with him in the ministry. Training was paramount to the pastor and would subsequently benefit those in the deacon ministry.

Chapter II

The literature review will show the research on leadership, women in the ministry, diversity in the pews, and non-denominationalism. The deacon training modules for this project were all customized to meet the needs of the specific ministry. Knowing who you are and how you got to where you are, remain critical pieces to a great puzzle. Having that knowledge is a basis for a solid review of the literature in this chapter. Research literature tended to focus on the office of the deacons. John Walker set the tone by defining the pastor's role in leadership and training. "The pastor is the spiritual and administrative head of the church. He is fully cognizant of the meditative help his sheep need and his deacon must be able to deliver."[6] The author correlated Jesus' teaching of the disciples with his teaching of the deacons at SJBC. While emphasizing the need for leaders to overflow with the fruit of the spirit, the researcher also encouraged the fruit to stand on a firm foundation. Otherwise, its life expectancy would be critically shortened. It is accomplishing the Master's purpose that is essential. The deacon will not be able to do so without the ingredients to grow in wisdom and stature, just as Jesus did. John Walker stated "the life and work of the deacon demands that casual reading be replaced by planned dedicated study."[7]

Chapter III

In this chapter is the basis of the model framed by theological vision. Training is inherent throughout the old and new testaments. Being scripturally sound in doctrine, the researcher believes the project is essential to a strong deacon training model (APPENDIX

---

[6] John H. Walker, *A Fresh Look at the New Testament Deacon Workbook* (Lithonia, GA: Orman Press, Inc., 2001), 16.

[7] Walker, 33.

A). Numbers 11:25 promotes that marriage of the spirit. Acts 6 traces and attacks the problem of ethnic and cultural diversity that accompanies the early church and provides a model for the 21st century church.[8] This model project confirms the need for the pastor and deacon to become one.

Chapter IV

The researcher identified several models that better reflected the needs of SJBC. After extensive investigation, the researcher selected methods and best practices to help shape this model project. These methods included observations, focused groups, pre- and post-assessments, and questionnaires. The end result was the creation of a deacon/pastor leadership model.

Chapter V

In Chapter V, the reader will understand the procedures and processes utilized in implementing this project. The field experience was approached with caution while being both methodologically sound and practical in nature. The initial steps in the field experience were both to recognize and address the hurts that the church family had endured, while simultaneously establishing the need for training and deacon/pastor partnership. Most importantly, the researcher listened and observed, but did not side with anyone regardless of who was right or wrong in dealing with church conflict. The pain was real. The need for training became more evident. However, the need for establishing a partnership with the pastor was even greater.

Chapter VI

It was apparent to the researcher that the spiritual knowledge levels of the deacons did not meet the needs of the church family. For a change to occur, this chapter would be

---

[8] McMickle, 9.

the conduit for an inevitable paradigm shift. Through this model, the leadership was

exposed to a new way of thinking and sharing the Gospel. This biblically-based model

began the process of challenging traditional mindsets regarding servant leadership. The

researcher discovered a more strategic means to train deacons while building a biblical

foundation and partnership through the ministry. Prayer undergirded the model and was

reflected throughout its implementation. A by-product of this model implementation was

the impact it had on the congregation as a whole and the deacon/pastor leadership.

Meeting the needs of the people became the driving force in being obedient to God's

plan. This was the catalyst that evoked a spiritual shift that changed the fabric of training

and worship at SJBC, leading to partnership of similar hearts.

CHAPTER I

MINISTRY FOCUS

The Spiritual Journey

As the researcher reflects on his spiritual journey, he recalls the events that have shaped who he is and who he will become. It is with that spiritual belief that his faith has been shaped and established. The researcher is fully molded as a Man of Faith, winning souls for Christ. This journey is laced with spirituality in all its dimensions. According to Wayne Muller, "Clearly, our lives of who we are, is powerfully influenced by the community from which I have come."[1]

The researcher grew up and was nurtured in a loving yet disciplined home with both parents. His paternal and maternal grandparents were present and active in the development of his life. A sense of family was evident this kind of environment. However, as life would have it, there was a major element of misfortune that occurred in the nucleus of this family structure. When the researcher was fifteen years of age, his mother and father divorced. His mother was very angry which left the family with mixed emotions. This was a major event that impacted the total family dynamics.

In the realm of marriage, his parents' bitter divorce taught the researcher how vulnerable all of us can be. It also taught him to be empathetic in his relationship with people's feelings and emotions. Recalling his parents' divorce had a significant impact on his perception of the foundation for a marriage.

---

[1] Wayne Muller, *How Then Shall We Live,* (New York, New York: Bantam Books, 1997), 41.

The Salvation Experience

In July of 1992, the researcher accepted Jesus Christ in his life. Four months later, the researcher entered into marriage with Cynthia Joann Adkins. His commitments continued in spending more time with God in studying His Word. During his devotional time, his preparation for teaching Sunday school, as well as his congregational Bible Study time, the researcher was fully under the leadership of his pastor and mentor. The researcher began to have an inward conviction of wanting to see others saved. The researcher later became cognizant that the burning desire to see others saved, along with his boldness to approach them, was the researcher's spiritual gift that God had so graciously given him.

Call to Ministry

In the development of knowing the researcher, Christ had matured and secured him. Since his salvation experience with Christ in July 1992, his love for music, outdoors, and people have intensified even the more. That is why living his life knowing that the researcher will die is the absolute expression of the reality of why the researcher must work while it is day, for the night will come when no man can work.[2] Night time may not necessarily be the chronological bodily removal from the existential, but an illness or unexpected tragedy that could leave him in a paralytic state, preventing him from doing what the researcher loves and from doing what God has assigned him to do on this earth.

---

[2] John 9:4 New International Version (NIV).

Philippians 2:13 states, "For it is God who works in you to will and to act according to his good purpose."[3] This inspired word became his conviction and inspiration that would allow him the privilege to preach his initial sermon. Unexpectedly, this preaching privilege had begun to open doors of opportunity to not only preach, but to see God transform the lives of people through this earthen vessel. As this conviction would increase, so would the burden of wanting to maintain those new converts that would accept Christ. Writing sermons required more study time with God. Preaching youth revivals during the week and preaching on the weekends began to impose on the researcher's fulltime job of thirteen years at that time. Like Nehemiah, the researcher was blessed to have the stability of a secure job. The current conditions and plight of his people became so sorrowful to him. Something needed to be done that would give God's people hope. After much prayer in seeking some direction from God on what to do at this juncture in his ministry, God began to soften his heart right in the geographical area of where the researcher was doing much of his preaching. The Eastern Shore of Virginia (E.S.V.A.) became the place where God had given the researcher a passion and compassion to do his work. In 1999, the former pastor of Shiloh Baptist Church shared a vision that the researcher would be their next Pastor. After much prayer by both pastor and people, this became a reality that would last for twelve years. The researcher's assignment there was completed in May, 2011.

The Call to SJBC

A very good pastor friend of the researcher informed him that the SJBC had been without a pastor for three years, and in need of pastoral leadership. Knowing the researcher's heart for God's people, he discerned that the researcher would be a perfect

---

[3] Philippians 2:13.

match for this congregation. In October 2010, the researcher applied, underwent the vetting process, and by His grace, God entrusted the SJBC family to the researcher to pastor and lead.

Upon arrival at SJBC, the researcher observed needs he believed could further enhance the worship and serving experience, specifically for the deacons, but just as important for the church itself and the greater community that SJBC served. Those needs were categorized into three main areas: The Needs of the Deacons, Needs of the Church and finally, the Needs of the Community. This environmental scan would supply necessary information in the development of the needed training model.

Needs of the Deacons

The researcher was most impressed by the number of deacons who were actively involved in Sunday School. Of the eighteen deacons, approximately 80% were regular and consistent attendees. This was perceived as strength reflective in the ministry. However, there were other areas that needed attention in order that the church continued to progress toward meeting several challenges. Due to the fragmentation of both the church itself and its leadership, the researcher felt strongly that he had to establish a close relationship with those who had been 'in charge' while being without a pastor. There was dissension among the ranks, both internally among the deacons and externally among the congregation. Even the community was affected.

For many years, as shared by the deacons, 'they handled the business of the church.' It was evident that that statement was true. There seemed to be no 'God-talk' or spirituality shown from some in the deacon ministry. In fact, many of the deacons consistently sat in the pastor's office during the morning worship services and only exited when it was time for offering or altar call. Previously, this had been the acceptable

practice due to not having a safe place downstairs to count the money generated.

Counting the money during the worship hour provided more 'protection.' However, as

time went by, the practice evolved into some deacons not participating in the worship

experience. Rather, they continued to count the money and have impromptu and

unofficial meetings.

The greater challenge, however, seemed to be the lack of organized and regular

training on matters that affected the worship experience and could delay or deny meeting

the needs of the congregation and community. These matters included, but were not

limited to the following: Counseling the Non-Traditional Congregant, Ministering to the

Sick, Rightly Dividing the Word, and many other areas. The researcher envisioned

change would only occur through prayer and training.

Spiritual Matters in the 21st Century: Offering Godly Counsel

The deacon ministry needed to have the ability to offer godly counsel to the non-

traditional congregant. The church was growing. Non-traditional families and atypical

situations were a part of worship experience. Same sex households were represented in

the pews. Generational patterns of teen pregnancy were prevalent. Gang members'

influence outside of the church walls was attempting to interact with the church's

teenagers within the church. Never before had leadership needed to be abreast in handling

more in-depth societal ills within the walls of the church. Within the church community,

poverty is pervasive. Carol Dashiff, et al. states, "Chronic exposure to poverty increases

adolescents' risks for mental disorders such as depression, behavior risk such as substance use (Fergusson, et. al., 2000), early sexual debut (McBride, Paikoff, and Holmbeck, 2003), and criminal activity (Davis, Banks, Fisher and Grudzinsksa, 2004)."[4]

Spiritual Matters in the 21st Century: Ministering to the Sick

This was the job most often performed by the clergy at SJBC. Deacons were now being asked to lay hands on the sick. They could pray, but could they pray the prayer of faith? Therein lies the paradox. Young and old parishioners and/or their family members with complex and chronic medical issues (AIDS, Hepatitis C, etc.) were calling out to the elders for prayer. Going to homes and hospitals where they had to be fully gowned and masked was beginning to be a monthly occurrence. Churches are informal service providers especially while ministering to the elderly. The researcher has consistently demonstrated the "vital role that clergy and congregations play in the lives of older adults."[5]

Spiritual Matters in the 21st Century: Rightly Dividing the Word

Deacons were being called upon to act as lay-pastors. It was essential they had the tools and knowledge to rightly interpret and share scripture. No longer could they depend on what they had heard from their parents and others. They now had to know the Word for themselves. Regardless of the environment or situation they found themselves, it was critically important that they were fully armored from head to toe. Retreating was not an option. They couldn't just know the Bible but they had to know the author as well. J. O. Sanders (2007) states "churches grow in every way when they are guided by strong,

---

[4] Carol Dashiff et al. "Poverty and Adolescent Mental Health," *Journal of Child and Adolescent Psychiatric Nursing* 22 (Feb. 2009), 25 accessed March 9, 2015 http://www.onlinelibrary.wiley.com.

[5] James W. Ellor and Michael E. Sherr, "Elder Mistreatment and the Church: Potential Roles for Helping Professionals and Congregations," *Social Work and Christians* 36 (2009):23, accessed March 9, 2015, http://www.nacsw.org.

spiritual leaders with the touch of the supernatural radiating in their service."[6] Through

the Holy Spirit and in partnering with the pastor through training, the deacon's ability to

rightly divide the Word was on its way to fruition. Bible Study, Sunday School, and other

learning environments would be key elements.

Needs of the Church

By the time the pastor arrived in May 2011, SJBC had been without a pastor in

excess of three years. Disagreements were points of contention. As a result, some of the

sheep scattered. Relationships had been severely strained and trust died. At this point,

healing and forgiveness was the only option. Michael Firmin and Jonathan Young argue

that, "in ministry context, trust relationships with congregants and church leaders play an

important role."[7] In light of being without a pastor, SJBC needed to be healed. The

researcher recognized this breach within the first few months of his pastorate. There was

a need to plan strategic ways to address the tear. There was a dire need to preach and

teach on healing. Otherwise, the ability to evangelize would be thwarted. He also

recognized the church had no vision, no direction. SJBC was in the "survival" mode.

Operating for years without a pastor was, to say the least, one of the most costly

experiences the church, itself, had gone through. The cost was not just in the day to day

operations, it was not in the brick and mortar, but souls were at stake, too. The researcher

had to help the church build capacity in its leadership and throughout the church as a

whole. The building of capacity also included the immediate staff that was in need of

---

[6] J. Oswald Sanders *Spiritual Leadership: A Commitment to Excellence for Every Believer* (Chicago, IL: Moody 2007), Google e-book.

[7] Michael W. Firmin and Jonathan W. Young, "Qualitative Perspectives Toward Relational Connection in Pastoral Ministry, Qualitative Report19 (2014):1, accessed February 3, 2015, http://www.nova.edu.ssss/QR/QR19/young93.pdf.

more specialized training, in order to more effectively execute their job requirements. They attended monthly meetings with the pastor. As importantly, the eleven associate ministers were at various stages in their own abilities to preach, teach and lead. One associate minister had previously been a pastor at another church. Of the remaining ten, all but two had attended some seminary. All attended monthly trainings with the pastor.

While recognizing the needs of the church, the researcher would be remiss if he did not include the need for the deaconess to be far more active in the ministry. Traditionally, they were responsible for preparing communion, baptism, attending funerals and wearing their famous white attire on the first Sunday of each month. The researcher would spend endless hours with the deacons, but very few with the deaconess. Similarly, as their male counterparts, the deaconess also lacked training. As the researcher envisioned, it would be necessary for the deaconess concept to eventually evolve into a true diaconate ministry.

Needs of the Community

Being that SJBC was located in the heart of four separate and distinct housing developments, the needs surrounding them were tremendous (APPENDIX B). In Smith Homes, the closest housing development nearest the church, single mother head of households represent 44.9% of the families. Fifty percent of the residents have less than a high school education. The median income in 2011 was $13,370 yearly as compared to $39,637 for the city of Greensboro[8]. Research has revealed the need to establish a more intimate relationship within the community confines to begin stopping the hemorrhage.

---

[8] *Smith-Homes Neighborhood in Greensboro, NC* accessed March 15, 2015, http://www.city-data.com/neighborhhod/Smith-Homes-Greensboro, NC.html.

Some of the ministries at SJBC seemed to have become irrelevant to those social ills. It was barely meeting the needs of the people.

After establishing a relationship with community leaders, the researcher felt it not robbery to establish a Vacation Bible School within one of the housing developments. The researcher opened the church doors to those individuals in the community who were not members, but needed a place to worship and at times, bury their dead. The body of Christ is formed of people who belong to the Christian community, redeemed by Him who is the head of the church. This community represents different parts of the body, where each of them have different functions, 'yet they are bound together in a common sharing and loving relationship'.

SJBC had always had the good reputation in the Greensboro community. Efforts to expand that reputation and influence would start with a basic door hanger inviting people to church, Sunday School, and participating in a community give-away (clothing appliances, toys, etc.) which served as an evangelism tool. The researcher believed that when he got them inside the church there would be a great opportunity to help them see Christ.

A Need for Collaboration

SJBC had been a respectable force within the community for over one hundred years. The church served as a place of refuge for the homeless, provided an established child care facility, and homes for the elderly and poor. Unfortunately, somewhere along the line, the church had gotten off track: there were areas that needed right-siding, re-envisioning, dusting off, discarding and re-shaping. The researcher discovered that the 28 committees of the church had mission statements, but the church itself did not. It was imperative that these so called committees transformed into ministries. A grassroots effort to remedy this issue was developed. The Vision Team made up of former members of the Pastoral Search Committee helped develop the Mission and Vision Statements. As a result, the researcher met quarterly with the ministry presidents to keep abreast and informed of ministry needs and challenges. This shared partnership helped him to set and monitor expectations inherent in the ministry. As a result, better communication occurred among and between the ministries. Additionally, the researcher could help identify training needs collectively and individually among the ministries.

Part of that more effective communication resulted in a church calendar for the year. Everyone would now know what was happening at the church in one single glance. The church was now becoming a pastor-led church, not a deacon run one. The pendulum had begun to swing more in an aligned position. Both pastor and deacon were now collaborating together.

The young adults, ages 18-35, had grown fewer and fewer. Efforts to begin a Young Adult Only Bible Study, Young Adult Praise Team and a Young Adult Revival were implemented as a means to re-define their importance. Their very existence depended on the ability to invite them back into the fold and be a strong part of that fold.

Urgency for Ministry and Training

Based on the information shared, it has become even more urgent for leadership in the African-American church to align their thinking with the changing needs in today's church, while it is day. As Romans 12:1-2 states, "I beseech you therefore brethren by the mercies of God, that ye present your bodies a living sacrifice, Holy, acceptable unto God which is your reasonable service. And be not conformed to this world, but be ye transformed by the renewing of your mind. That ye may prove what is good, and acceptable, and perfect, will of God." [9] It is in this transformative scripture that give rise to the Great Commission, which commands us to go into the world preaching the gospel. [10] When SJBC servant leaders 'go' into the world, they will be exposed to the rapid decline of the African-American family and social ills that impact family values and structures. "The world as we know it today suffers from an increase in moral disparity. Our families have become fragmented by life's circumstances causing something once considered as sacred and safe entry, have been regulated to a blend of options and lifestyles. Drugs, alcohol and violence have invaded our schools, communities and families." [11]

As importantly, the researcher is not only committed, but obligated to affect the mindsets of the church leaders. As in Numbers 11:17, it states in part, "I will come down and talk with thee there and I will take of the spirit which is upon thee and will put it upon them and they shall bear the burden of the people with thee, that thou bear it not thyself alone." [12] This aspect of ministry is driven by Muller's quote, "If we feel ashamed of whom we are, we will pretend to be someone else." [13] There is no room in his ministry or in him for arrogance or shame to reside. The researcher must be his authentic self, according to James H. Harris who referenced Miles Jones' work. [14] His ministry must be

---

[9] Romans 12:1-2.

[10] Matthew 28:16-20.

[11] Simmons.

[12] Numbers 11:17.

[13] Muller, 43.

[14] James H. Harris *The Word Made Plain* (Minneapolis: Augsburg Fortress, 2004), 39.

just as authentic. The researcher want to always be approachable because it demonstrates to leadership the burden Christ created in him so that it may flow from his heart to theirs. It is through this partnership of hearts and minds that the church is strengthened. Doing what the researcher loves bring new learning practices to his ministry and provides another opportunity to teach that to the leaders. 'The needs of the people in the 21st century are crying out to the church for solutions to the very present problems.' This remedy will only come through prayer, intentional instruction and spiritual development.

Ministerial Strengths and Challenges

Effectively functioning in his ministerial context has its strengths and challenges. The researcher strengths are: an unusual faith (resignation from a secure position to accept a first-time, less paying pastorate), ability to adapt to a changing environment (through the Spirit, he came away as an "immigrant" to live among the natives, adapting to a new culture), and strength to establish structure to mobilize people in the ministry, (an unusual faith practice that has sustained him through the years of his ministry). The researcher's faith in Christ keeps him focused and cognizant of his calling. It has allowed him to accomplish great things for God's glory and has allowed him to take advantage of preparing himself to do even greater work for our Lord and Savior. This lets the researcher know that God is still with him. Psalms 116:12 reads "How can I repay the Lord for all His goodness to me?"

The challenge of trying to establish structure and mobilize people into ministry positions can sometimes result in the pastor doing most of the work. This sometimes forces him into the role of what Edward P. Wimberly, a leading theologian and author, calls as an "over-functioner."[15] According to Wimberly, wherever there is an over-functioner there is an under-functioner. Over-functioning is a role assigned to a family member in which he is only valued if he performs a certain role.[16] The harvest is plentiful, but the workers are few, according to Matthew 9:37.[17] When people do not step up to their ministry responsibilities, it leaves the work undone. He has learned to set parameters and carefully choose when to give of his time with limited involvement. His time has become too important for him to conduct ministry alone. That is why lay-leaders also must be trained and developed. It necessitates another opportunity to teach leadership when to step up and even when to step back. These ideals are why it is essential for the deacon/pastor relationship to be one of progressive thinking, action and interaction.

Influential Spiritual Gifts

There are two images that have shaped the researcher as a minister and pastor. The first image that shaped him as a minister is the pastor that God has strategically placed in his life. The Reverend Dr. Dwight Riddick has been the spiritual leader and influence for him. After he joined the Gethsemane Baptist Church in July 1992 at the age of 30, Pastor Riddick baptized, married, licensed him to preach, ordained and installed him where he presently serves as pastor. While maintaining his own identity, the researcher tries to emulate his pastor's integrity, humility, and role as he carried himself as a respectable pastor, husband, father and mentor. As God gave the priest Eli as a gift to Samuel, so has he given the researcher his pastor as a gift to assist him in developing

---

[15] Edward P. Wimberly *Recalling Our Own Stories; Spiritual Renewal for Religious Caregivers* (San Francisco: Josey Bass, 1997), 59.

[16] Ibid.

[17] Matthew 9:37.

him as a minister, while mentoring him as a son in the ministry. For this, he is forever grateful.

The other half of the research is impacted by what God promised in October of 1992, as to what He would do for him upon rendering his commitment to his Father's will. That promise was manifested within the following two years. God saved the researcher's father and paternal grandfather. The researcher was able to witness both of their baptisms. This was confirmation in his life that "being confident of this, that he who began a good work in you will carry it on to completion until the day of Christ Jesus."[18] A few years later, the researcher's grandfather died in Christ and the researcher was blessed to be allowed by his pastor to preach his very first funeral. The researcher's father is still in church and is faithful to the ministry. These significant events have had a major impact on his image as a minister. It motivates him to preach, it encourages him to be patient with people and it inspires him every time that he is challenged by life's circumstances.

The researcher believes that his salvation experience with God radiates in him through his posture as a minister. The researcher believes that the people, family circumstances that have taken place beyond his control, the places and the timing of the ecclesiastical call on his life, all play a strategic role in what his gift is to the family of the earth. Wayne Muller likened "the gift" as to a seed. "Some were planted during our lifetime and some transmitted by our parents, our ancestors and our society."[19] It is what can grow out from the seed that is impressive. On the outside that gift may not look impressive. It may not dress impressively, or even fit into a certain social classification

---

[18] Philippians 1:6.

[19] Muller, 79.

that is impressive. The one distinction that the researcher has is that he is an asset to the kingdom of God and therefore, a gift to the flock and community, at large.

Ministerial Context

The researcher's current assignment is at the historic St. James Baptist Church (SJBC) in Greensboro, North Carolina. Arriving in Greensboro in May 2011, this promised to be a significant opportunity to minister to some great people. The city of Greensboro has a population of over 275,879, based on 2012 census data[20] (APPENDIX C). It is the third largest city in North Carolina with five major colleges within a ten-mile radius of the church community (APPENDIX D).

SJBC is situated in southeast Greensboro. The predominantly African-American church is surrounded by four low-income housing developments. However, the majority of the membership does not live in the housing development community. Yet, the community fully embraces the church as its own. The church was always active in the civil rights movement in Greensboro. Former Pastor Prince Graves pastored SJBC for forty-five years and was a one-term City Councilman with tremendous influence throughout Greensboro proper. His influence caused many decisions to be reviewed and/or changed, as he and others deemed in the best interest of the African-American people. Rev. Graves was considered "an institution" to and in the community. Under his leadership, SJBC went from a small church on a red clay hill with less than thirty-five members, to a church at the height of his ministry serving over a thousand. Pastor Graves was then followed by Pastor Vernon C. King, nephew of Dr. Martin Luther King, Jr. The church continued to grow.

---

[20] City of Greensboro, *Living* accessed December 29, 2014 www.greensboro-nc.gov/.

Currently, the 101 years old church serves 800 members, with weekly Sunday services at 7:45 a.m. and 11:00 a.m. Congregants average age span is 50-59 years, with 40% deemed professionals living in the surrounding communities.[21] This group represents approximately 60% of the membership.[22] SJBC has approximately 30% of its membership under the age of 40 years. Children and youth, (ages 0-18), comprise 10% of the membership.[23] The church's culture is very traditional but cautiously transitioning towards a more progressive mindset. Still perceived somewhat cavalier in leadership access, the church is being challenged toward a more 21st century thinking mode. The final authority for decision-making is still male- dominated but, the tide is changing. The church is evolving into a more balanced, greater and active involvement of women in the overall operations of its membership. Sixty percent of the congregation is female.[24] This female majority will be one of the bases for the consideration of the implementation of a future diaconate ministry at SJBC.

Upon arrival at this historic church, it was obvious the church was in need of tremendous healing. At that time, the church had been without a pastor for about three years. The former pastor had died unexpectedly. Prior to his death, the deacon board had been in a divisive struggle with the pastor. As a result, the church ended up becoming two distinct factions: one side not trusting the other yet worshipping together every Sunday morning with smiles and hearts heavy. Based on the church's Constitution, the deacon board was placed in charge to administer the daily operations of the church and

---

[21] SJBC Church *Archives*.

[22] Ibid.

[23] Ibid.

[24] Ibid.

supply the pulpit until God sent a pastor.[25] It was during these times that the deacon board, as a whole, had its strengths and opportunities for growth on public display. These challenges were real. The deacons were now operating in a sphere in which they were not accustomed. The church was in the spiritual battle of its life.

The Missing Link

SJBC has always had a very strong Sunday School. Effective Christian education has continued to be the foundation upon which the ministries were established. The church primarily focused its ministries on the seniors, women, men, youth and children. The missing piece was ministering to the needs of the young adults ages 18-35. Not even a Sunday School class was designed for these Young Adults. College students returning home always returned to the Teen Class, their former class. A class was later established for the Young Adults; however, the latter aged young adults (26 -35) with children were addressed, not the younger age span without children. The deacons were informed; however, efforts to address this need yielded very little. Leadership had missed an opportunity to serve an important part of the membership. As Hammett and Pierce stated in their book, *Reaching People Under 40, While Keeping People Over 60,* "Many churches and even denominations, have not yet figured out that we are in a different culture and that if we don't change things, we are not going to reach younger generations".[26]

The last two pastors at SJBC operated in their own strengths while conducting ministry. They appealed to a more traditional congregant that emphasized the reason for

---

[25] SJBC Church Constitution ratified and amended, 2012.

[26] Edward H. Hammett and James R. Pierce, *Reaching People under 40 while Keeping People over 60* (St. Louis, Missouri: Chalice Press, 2007), 30.

salvation. Current membership wants that and much more. Members have reported a desire to go deeper into the Word. Like James Emery White, in his book, *Re-thinking the Church,* they want a method of communicating the Gospel that must change according to the language, culture and background of the audience."[27] The pastor and the deacon had to now serve a full course meal encompassing the same great message, but do so using different tools. Both pastor and deacon had to function as one entity together, in order to accomplish this goal.

Community Impact

SJBC continues to be a mover and shaker in the Greensboro community. The church established the first homeless shelter in its fellowship hall.[28] As a result, Urban Ministry saw the need and later started its own. The church even had Social Services assistance through church members with that expertise. For reasons and causes like this, St. James Baptist Church is best known. Training for the deacon ministry now had to align with even more progressive thinking and service. Over the years, demographics had impacted how things were done in the life and needs of the church. Those changing demographics continue to be one of the reasons the church can no longer operate with business as usual.

Deacon Ministry Addressed by Model

The particular area of ministry that the researcher has chosen to address is that of training of the deacon ministry. When the researcher first encountered the deacon ministry at SJBC, he was able to detect and observe that there was substantial evidence portraying lack of spirituality and poor communication among the deacon leadership and

---

[27] James Emery White. *Re-thinking the Church* (Grand Rapids, MI: Baker Books, 1997), 39.

[28] SJBC Church Archives.

congregation. Meetings were focused primarily on the business aspects of the church with little emphasis on spirituality. Also during the observation process, the researcher noted the deacon board members average age was about 10 years his senior. There were no planned facilitations of workshops and opportunities for training and spiritual development or even a mention of ministry progression. Additionally, collaboration between pastor and deacon was not as developed as it needed to be. It was at this pivotal juncture that the researcher envisioned the development of a training model for the deacon ministry had to be planned, developed and further strengthened in order to deliver an effective and quality program for them.

Marvin A. McMickle states "Yet the question that remains is whether our churches today are operating with an understanding of the work of the deacon that is informed primarily by Scripture rather than by recent history and traditions."[29] The researcher concurs with McMickle in that the deacons primarily based their work off of the history and traditions of SJBC and not necessarily based on what thus said the Lord. The researcher believes that it is critical for the deacon to operate and function in a capacity that coincides with scripture.

Model Justification

There was a lack of sensitivity to being attentive to the spiritual and physical needs of the pastor so that he may minister effectively to the congregation. Those spiritual needs were as simple as praying for and with him before he went out to the people to lead them through worship and preaching while also leading the un-churched to

---

[29] McMickle, 53.

Jesus Christ. Those physical needs included making sure that the researcher was cared for and not distracted so he could minister fully by the Holy Spirit.

All of the aforementioned situations have played a major determining factor in his rationale for incorporating and developing the training model for the deacon ministry for SJBC. Accordingly, McMickle's question regarding whether churches are operating with an understanding of the work of the deacon with regards to scripture versus recent history and tradition is relevant.[30] Keeping that question in mind that McMickle presented, the researcher was led to carefully and deliberately develop and train deacons and deaconesses so that churches, in particular SJBC, can prepare and equip persons to serve in a way that is consistent with the biblical model of *"diakonos"* or servant leadership.[31]

Another rationale for designing a model for developing and training deacons and deaconesses was that there was minimal formal training for the present deacons and deaconesses upon my arrival. Due to the paradigm shift of the face of the church and the perplexity of problems that parishioners were challenged with, it was imperative that the deacon ministry embody the changing dynamics of the work of the deacons and deaconesses. Rather, this paradigm shift now requires the deacon ministry to demonstrate efficiency far beyond counting money to ministering to souls while serving the needs of SJBC.

Deacon training for SJBC was essential to breathing life back into a ministry that was then on life support. It was imperative that not only leadership, but the entire church family heard from the man of God as to his vision for the church. Facilitating trainings that were congruent to both the vision and needs of the church was one of the earlier lines

---

[30] Ibid.

[31] Ibid, 54.

of defense during the transition. It was also critical that the pastor taught with authority and confidence as he led the leadership through being re-taught and, in some instances, being taught for the first time.

CHAPTER II

LITERATURE REVIEW

Chapter II presents a literature review on leadership, diversity in the pews which includes women in leadership, non-denominationalism, and a collaborative partnership between deacons and pastor. It also includes other models that reflect a quality deacon training program. Deacons are called to be versatile in their functions as servant leaders. No longer can they just relate to the traditional congregant, but they must embrace the diverse people and needs in the sanctuary, including a positive relationship with the pastor. In so doing, there must be a partnership of similar hearts reflective throughout this model. Each of the training models presented in this project at St. James Baptist Church (SJBC), represents a unique and distinct characteristic emphasized by this particular ministry. Some of the characteristics of the 21st century church are further described below.

21st Century Ministry

We have been living in the 21st century now for fifteen years. Many people, including church-goers, however, think advanced technology has been the 21st century tool that has shaped the world. Society has moved from the black and white picture tube to the LED internet television to the curved LED display. The church has also gone through a similar metamorphosis evolving from one room (such as the original SJBC) to mega-churches without denominations. "There is no single design for 21st century churches. The next generations will develop innovative ways to be effective in the third millennium,"[1] according to researcher, Leith Anderson. The sense of community is far more diverse and less defined. "The pastor is the spiritual and administrative head of the church. As spiritual leader, he is to teach and preach the Gospel and provide leadership in developing the various ministries necessary, as God directs him," according to Dr. John H. Walker in his workbook, *A Fresh Look at the New Testament Deacon*.[2] It is God's intention that the "spiritual offices of deacon and pastor work together cooperatively, not against each other."[3] Deacons historically have received on the job training. For many years that type of training has sufficed. However, recently the need for more specialized Christian Education for the body has evolved. According to Dr. James Taylor "The perspective of churches serving large numbers of people who stand in need of meditative help certainly includes the deacon at the forefront."[4] These are but a few of the changes presented in the 21st century affecting the church community.

Characteristics of the 21st Century Church: Technological Connectivity

Twenty-first century churches have many characteristics. For this project, key characteristics discussed will be: Technological Connectivity, Diversity in the Pews, Non-Denominationalism and Women in Leadership. The researcher believes these characteristics are essential elements for fully understanding the place of the church and its leadership in relevant training and support. For example, today's church is losing

---

[1] Leith Anderson, "What Will the 21st Century Church Be Like?" *Enrichment Journal,* accessed March 18, 2015 http://enrichmentjournal.ag.org/200001/026_21stcentury.cfm.

[2] Walker, 16.

[3] Steve Lemke, "How Deacons Can Help their Pastors," *Baptist Message* June 11, 2009, accessed March 15, 2015 http://www.baptistcenter.net.

[4] Dr. James Taylor, *Equipping Laity for Servant Leadership* (Bloomington, IN: Author House, 2009), 47.

members from ages 18-35 years. Those who do attend, see church as a "refuge from a constantly plugged in existence,"[5] according to Seth Tower Hurd, author of "The Unexpected Things Millennials Want in Church." However, their use of social media is a constant, daily, almost moment by moment activity. The connectedness of the church allows them to use their cell phones, iPads, and tablets to access the Word of God. Not only can the Word of God be accessed, but also Christian literature, gospel music and plays instantaneously. However, the members, ages 18-35, still "have a very dim view of church and very skeptical of religion."[6] Any means to bridge that disconnect is critical for the 21st century church.

Diversity in the Pews

Kathy Moore Cowan states "By now, we all know we are in the midst of a tsunami. In just seven short years, the number of Americans age 65 and older will increase by 65 percent, from 35 million to 55 million. By 2050, there will be 88 million Americans in this age group, representing one in every five Americans."[7] These baby boomers are those at the retirement years who become less active many times in the church community. "The church must meet the needs of four different generational groups from Builders (born prior to 1945) to Boomers (born 1945-1964) to Busters and

---

[5] Seth Tower Hurd, "The Unexpected Things Millennials Want in Church," *Relevant Magazine* (November 2014): accessed March 18, 2015 http://www.relevantmagazine.com/god/church/unexpected-things-millenials-want-church.

[6] Marian V. Liautaud, "5 Things Millennials Wish the Church Would Be," *Exponential*, accessed March 18, 2015, http://www.exponential.org/5-things-millennials-wish-the-church-would-be/.

[7] Kathy Moore Cowan, "The Graying of America: Preparing for What Comes Next," *Federal Reserve Bank of St. Louis,* accessed March 18, 2015 https://www.stlouisfed.org/publications/bridges/fall-2013/the-graying-of-america-preparing-for-what-comes-next.

Generation X (born 1965-1983) to Millennials (born since 1984)."[8] Inclusive in the diverse congregations are members with alternative lifestyles that require ministering just as any other member. These lifestyles include same sex marriage and various family structures as well as persons who are un-churched or have strayed away from church who are considered backsliders.

Non-Denominational Influence

Today's 21st century church is moving toward more non-denominations. "In the past century, denominationalism was a very large part of what it meant to be Christian. Growing numbers of churches might be characterized as open systems, attempting to embrace everyone while imposing little on anyone."[9] Traditionally, churches were defined by their respective faith-base; one was Baptist or Methodist or Pentecostal, Catholic or COGIC. If the church remains denominational, then it becomes imperative that its membership know why it is Baptist or Methodist, etc. Inherent in the researcher's model are sessions establishing that knowledge base.

Women in Leadership

One of the characteristics of the 21st century church is the inclusion of women in leadership. The church must have women as a critical part of the leadership ministry. "Women should be able to serve the church in whatever positions they are qualified to

---

[8] Global Christian Center, "Challenges for the Twenty-First Church," accessed March 18, 2015 https://globalchristiancenter.com/administrative-leadership/church-leadership/church-leadership/25079-challenges-for-the-21st-century-church.

[9] Robert Wuthnow, "Church Realities and Christian Identity in the 21st Century," *Religion-online. The Christian Century*, May 12, 1993, 520-523 accessed March 18, 2015 http://www.religion-online.org /showarticles.asp?title=231.

fill,"[10] according to materials as indicated on the Christian Bible Reference website. Those who oppose women in ministry often cite Old Testament scripture where women were described as subservient by pointing to the New Testament scripture where Jesus' choice of men as apostles allegedly proves that point for a few believers.[11]

Need for Training

In the field, theologians recognize that church leaders, particularly deacons should continually train and re-train. However, churches across the country neglect to adequately train its leadership, particularly the deacon, who is charged primarily with ministering to and addressing the diverse needs of the congregation. SJBC sends its members, primarily the Sunday School teachers, to their local High Point Educational and Missionary Baptist Association and National Baptist Congress of Christian Education (HPEMBA) for continual training (APPENDIX E). Deacons were not actively involved in any of those structured trainings. As a result, less structured, almost fly-by-night, training was given to the deacon. The researcher was unsure if some of the deacons did not find the training necessary. For these reasons, it was necessary to implement a training model to facilitate their spiritual growth and development.

The training model came as a result of examination of the role of the pastor in relations to enabling and equipping God's leaders for training and ministry work. Training sessions were developed to emphasize the deacon's functions and responsibilities in the ministry. It was imperative that a collaborative partnership with the pastor be a critical part of the model's design. SJBC's model consisted of 46 sessions

---

[10] Christian Bible Reference Site, "What does the Bible Say about Women in Ministry", *Christian Bible Reference* accessed March 18, 2015 http://www.christianbiblereference.org/faq_women.htm.

[11] Ibid.

covering multi-years of instruction. Once the pastor was called and in place, the deacons focused their attention on hearing from one voice for preaching, teaching, training and leading. That voice was the voice of the pastor. Therefore, at SJBC, training was vital. Having the pastor initially deliver the training, while simultaneously building capacity within the deacon ministry, would be crucial.

The training models selected by the researcher were varied. These models were chosen by the researcher because of their similar training approaches and their practical nature of application upon which their foundations were built. The training models chosen represented urban settings, small to large church sizes, various levels of innovation established in the church, congregational involvement and various denominations or non-denominations.

Deacon Models Explored

"We live in a changing world and the church will either change to continue to spread the changeless truth of the gospel or it will die," states Aubrey Malphurs.[12] John Maxwell concurs, "If change does not cost you anything, then it is not real change."[13] The researcher, therefore, has explored five deacon ministries. As a result of needed change, they have varying degrees of a deacon/pastor-led training models for continued deacon ministry growth. They are: Deacon Ministries of Ebenezer Baptist Church Atlanta, Georgia, Love and Faith Community Church in Greensboro, North Carolina, Shalom Community Church of Greensboro, North Carolina, the Orthodox Presbyterian Church Deacon Model, Franklin Square, New York and Aubrey Malphurs' Training

---

[12] Aubrey Malphurs, *Being Leaders: The Nature of Authentic Christian Leadership* (Grand Rapids, MI: Baker Book House Company, 2006), 82.

[13] John Maxwell, *The Difference Maker* (Nashville, TN: Thomas Nelson Publishing, 2006), 90.

Leaders Model (APPENDIX F). Other ministerial programs were reviewed; however, the researcher believed they did not have a diagnostic and prescriptive plan of structure for the needed training that clearly represented the needs of SJBC.

Ebenezer Baptist Church Deacon Training Model

Ebenezer Baptist Church (EBC) tends to have a comprehensively planned deacon training model. The church while understanding the unique role the deacons played in ministry found it reasonable and prudent to incorporate a training program for the deacon. Scripturally based training sessions are determined by the pastor and chairman of the deacon ministry. The sessions are based on needs reflective in the ministry. Initial education sessions focus on the role of the deacons. The deacon training series used at EBC include: Ordinances of the Church, Black Baptist Church History, EBC Church History, EBC Governance, Equipped to Serve Ministry and EBC and its Future.[14] Each one of these sessions can last two to three weeks depending on questions and the information generated during the sessions. Each deacon is required, as part of his service, to fully attend and participate in each of these sessions. The pastor and other leaders conduct each of the ninety-minute sessions, lasting over the period of one year. The deacon has in-depth, yet frank discussions on the topic areas. Dr. Shellie Sampson, Jr. in his book, *Superior Leadership in Challenging Situations* states "no curriculum, no training format, no vision of ministry, no anticipation of people's needs and Christian personality can be properly dealt with until leaders come to grips with what the kingdom

---

[14] Elliott Bryant, *Interview by Veronica Bryant*, Greensboro, NC, December 23, 2014.

of God looks like when it is present and functioning in the lives of God's servant people."[15]

These sessions are the initial foundation for deacon education. EBC's Deacon Board, consisting of fifty-three members, continues in the training model by incorporating this knowledgebase with additional service learning projects and volunteer hours. The philosophy is that the deacon must 'walk-out' their learning through these service projects. Additionally, the deacon members must document volunteer service hours.

Each year the ministry develops a theme. The 2015 theme is "A Year of Prayer and Service: Strengthening our Commitment to Individual Growth and Transformation." Even the theme denotes the necessity of understanding and being cognizant of individual self and spiritual improvement, while being cognizant of pressing knowledge of social issues. It is this type of cutting-edge practice that is necessary for an effective ministry for a 21st century congregation. In addition, three to four books are read and discussed and incorporated into the training modules. Book Studies have focused on the "Purpose Driven Life", "The Servant Leader", "Be a Leader", and "It is Not About Me". Leaders take a deacon leadership profile and a spiritual gift inventory (APPENDIX G). Each quarter at EBC the deacon has focused prayer. They pray for the church (1st quarter), community (2nd quarter), children (3rd quarter), and for the world (4th quarter). It is the philosophy of leadership that being fair, knowledgeable, and balanced can assist in providing quality spiritual delivery not only for the deacon's household, but for that of his church constituents. This model specifically esteems congregational care, provides

---

[15] Shellie Sampson, *Superior Leadership in Challenging Situations,* (Nashville,TN: Townsend Press, 1998), 39.

leadership and nurtures the servant leader. The overall goal of this intensive training is to provide leadership with tools to serve as a catalyst for encouraging the broader congregation to build on a strong foundation of service to God and the community.

Shalom Community Church Deacon Training Model

Another effective deacon training model is one from Shalom Community Church, Greensboro, North Carolina. This Disciples of Christ denomination church of 250 members strong has a much smaller congregation but is just as impactful as EBC. This church was planted in 1999 by its current pastor, Rev. Dr. Eric Cole.[16] Leadership consists of the Stewardship Ministry which includes the deacons as one of its components. The congregation is both served by elders and deacons. Elders, nor deacons, are elected. They are appointed by the pastor in concert with others in leadership. It is this partnership of leadership that is germane to the success of the ministry. The deacon ministry exists solely to exalt Christ, edify the believers, and evangelize the unsaved. The deacon cannot be lovers or promoters of self.[17]

Shalom Church's deacons are considered servants. As servants, the deacons go through a variety of training and education opportunities throughout January-December which is their fiscal year. Each month focuses on a specific, often one word promised manifestation with corresponding and relevant scriptures. Training includes such areas as: Prompting, Positioning, Receiving, Responding, Overcoming, Overtaking, Matching, Moving, Praying, Praising, Thanksgiving, and Triumphing. All the manifestations are designed to provoke the deacon to the action required and generated through the Holy

---

[16] *Shalom Community Church,* accessed February 16, 2015 www.http://www.shalomword.org.

[17] Eric Cole, *Interview by Veronica Bryant*, Greensboro, NC February 18, 2015.

Spirit. The deacon is required to be actively involved in this Word Ministry of Christian Education. They must live and breathe the promised manifestations and be able to share these promises with the zone congregants they cover.

According to John Maxwell, in his Leadership Bible, "Followers of Christ are to be leaders of men and live at a higher level."[18] Their voice is the voice and heart of the pastor. It is one voice generated by the Holy Spirit through the leadership of the pastor. The teaching of these manifestations is standard, yet far more than foundational as they transform the deacon to a totally different level. The quintessential philosophy behind the training in this Word Ministry is that the deacon be better able to go deeper in service through the knowledge, use and interpretation of a rhema word. Each year the church focuses on God's promises to his people. The diaconate ministry of Shalom is one of the major conduits by which it is shared.

Love and Faith Christian Fellowship Church Deacon Training Model

The third deacon education model is Love and Faith Christian Fellowship Church, also in Greensboro, NC. This vibrant, yet unconventional ministry prides itself in extensive training for all, but specifically training for those in the diaconate. After being observed for one year through various worship experiences and being a faithful and consistent tither for three years, the men and women are provided in-depth training in and on the scriptures. Pastor Michael Thomas is the primary teacher utilizing scripture to further substantiate and support the various duties and responsibilities of the diaconate. The pastor helps to shape the ministry design through collaboration.

The pastor and elders of the church establish and develop relevant Christian Education sessions, conducted as often as needed. The diaconate meets twice monthly.

---

[18] John Maxwell, *Maxwell Leadership Bible*, (Nashville, TN: Thomas Nelson, Inc., 2002), 1155.

The first meeting is church business. The second meeting is purely for training. Topics covered include Nurturing and Caring for the Sheep, Mental Health in the Pews, Word in Action, Bereavement Care, and Family Devotions. Love and Faith's diaconate uses zones, just as Shalom Church, to not only minister to their congregants, but also to make applicable the word to those who live there.[19] This partnership of similar hearts works together and has grown into a strong deacon ministry. This astute church body stays on the cutting-edge of in-depth ministry in order to transform lives. The education to the deacon is transformative, far more than foundational. It allows the deacon to truly minister to the hungry, the poor, the homeless, and to those searching. There has to be significant and sustained growth in every deacon as determined by the pastor and elders. The pastor's vision must be their vision. Deacons who embrace the pastor's vision can help the congregation see where the pastor is going. Dr. John Walker espouses, "When the congregation sees the pastor and deacons working together, this creates the climate needed to promote growth and harmony."[20] If the ministry or any part of it tends to be at a stalemate, then the ministry leaders re-direct themselves to fasting and prayer in order to hear what the Lord is saying. They hear from the Lord without preconceived notions as to what they must do, what they must know, and how they must transfer that spiritual base to those they have been assigned covering over.

Orthodox Presbyterian Church Deacon Training Model

Pastor William Shisko, pastor of Orthodox Presbyterian Church (OPC) of Franklin Square, New York promotes another effective model for deacon training. The

---

[19] Steve and Liz McKinnon, *Interview by Ellis Armstrong*, Greensboro, NC, January 14, 2015.

[20] Walker, 35.

six-week, lecture formatted training with discussion, focuses half its training on Christian Doctrine.[21] Deacon principles serve as a significant focus. These principles are all biblically based and serve as a foundation for the ministry. The final half of the training highlights the deacon as a man and as an officer. As an officer, the training is segmented into *General Considerations* and then, *Specific Applications*. Integrated throughout these trainings is the Westminster Confession of Faith which is the Presbyterian Church's standards for living, secondary to the Bible. The Bible is deemed the infallible rule of faith and practice. This training accentuates, for believers, that the deacon ministry is a great reflection of God's mercies shown to His people. For those who do not believe, it's God's goodness leading them to repentance.

Malphurs Leadership Training Model

The last model is from Aubrey Malphurs which is more for the laity than just the deacon ministry. The principles, however, are universal and correlate with effective measures to train the deacon. Leadership training occurs for all in such positions. The training examines what the Bible teaches about leadership and lastly, four essential values or competencies that must be reflective in ministry. They are: The Leader's Character, His Skills, His Knowledge and His Emotions. Malphurs' Model suggests the necessity for an "inward assessment for leadership".[22] David led his people with both integrity and skilled hands. This is the essence of what godly leadership should look like, an opportunity to look inwardly and outwardly.

---

[21] William Shisko, "A Training Program for Deacons," *Ordained Servant*, 9, (July 2000): 62-70, accessed February 13, 2015 http://www.opc.org/OS/html/V9/3c.html.

[22] Aubrey Malphurs, "Growing Leaders for Ministry in the 21st Century," *Enrichment Journal*, accessed March 12, 2015 http://enrichmentjournal.ag.org.

Challenges in a 21ˢᵗ Century Church

David Jeremiah [23] proposes that churches can experience grievance problems when they are in a stage of growth. SJBC experienced such grievances as the congregation and community murmured about not having their needs met. The church had historically been known as a benevolent evangelizing church, where it met the many needs of the church and the community. Outreach was strong and had been a successful means of bringing families to Christ.

Gifts in the Leadership

C. Peter Wagner promotes leaders knowing their gifts, in his book, *Discover Your Spiritual Gifts.* He purports, "You can have a gift without an office, but you cannot have an office without a gift."[24] Some of the deacons at SJBC were unaware of their spiritual gifts and how they could be utilized in ministry. It was imperative that a connection and self-awareness of those gifts went beyond their understanding of their traditional roles. As part of the deacon development, training was essential to show the impact their gifts had on meeting the needs of a changing church. As Marcus J. Borg and John Dominic Crossan state "this does not mean that some people were spiritually superior to others. Rather, there are a variety of spiritual gifts coming from the same Spirit."[25] SJBC's deacons were no different.

---

[23] David Jeremiah, *Acts: The Church in Action—The Forward Progress of the Church* (San Diego: Turning Point, 2006), 23.

[24] C. Peter Wagner, *Discover Your Gifts Spiritual Gifts* (Ventura, California: Regal Books, 2002).

[25] Marcus J. Borg and John Dominic Crossan, *The First Paul*, Harper One, New York, NY, 2009, 201.

Building Relationships: Pastor and Deacon

"When a man is accepted to the office of deacon, according to Kate Ward-Turner in her book, *Deacon Training,* he becomes a member of a team of which the Holy Spirit is the coach and the pastor is the quarterback . . . the partner concept."[26] In Chapter 2 of James F. Miller's book, *Go Grow Your Church! Spiritual Leadership for African-American Congregations,* suggests this be a practical theology. That practical theology places "pastor and people meeting each other where they find each other."[27] This fosters an intentional effort to build relationship while honestly assessing the training needs of the leadership. The deacons did not understand vision. They just understood addressing needs. SJBC existed over one hundred years, yet never had a stated or established common vision. Miller further suggests "It's true that people respond to vision, not need, but more importantly, people (deacons) must be prepared to understand vision. It begins with the pastor."[28] Pastor and deacons united can only cement a kingdom-building, people-centered, strong and effective ministry.

Principles and Practices

"All training principles and practices should reflect those of the Savior"[29] according to Aubrey Malphurs. SJBC's deacons needed to be trained before they could be deployed. This training would be undergirded with a biblical foundation that helped guide the church through the process, serving both to drive and direct its implementation.

---

[26] Kate Ward-Turner, 16.

[27] James F. Miller, *Go Grow Your Church! Spiritual Leadership for African-American Congregations* (Cleveland: The Pilgrim Press, 2008), 40.

[28] Miller, 41.

[29] Malphurs, 101.

While meeting the deacons where they were, there was a need to build upon and further secure the foundation upon which they stood.

Edifice Complex

Deacons at SJBC used considerable time ensuring the actual physical building was maintained. In so doing, they ensured lights were kept on, lawns mowed and the pulpit supplied with a preacher. All of these responsibilities occurred while the church was without a pastor. According to Simmons, "We all need to abandon the Edifice Complex."[30] The edifice complex is when leadership focuses on the physical structure versus the spiritual structure. "Buildings are seen as a means to an end, not an end in itself---not monuments to our man-made ego and acquisition of resources. The church must be an internal building rather than one where people just come to worship."[31]

Deacon to Deacon

Within the years of discord, previously sound relationships were now fragmented and distant. The deacon ministry itself was without harmony and suffered from mistrust. Dave McCollum suggests "The deacons' relationship with each other should resemble a "band of brothers."[32] When soldiers go into battle, a bond develops that is hard to explain. The brethren are to be one. SJBC was suffering from the after-effects of an embattled leadership and congregation. They were just deacons, not brothers. The relationship is one of accountability among and between the brethren. With the pastor leading the charge, that accountability is reciprocated. According to Jim Henry, cited in

---

[30] Simmons, accessed March 3, 2015.

[31] Ibid.

[32] Dave McCollum, "The Rewards of a Deacon," *Lancaster Baptist Church*, accessed March 3, 2015 http://www.ministry127.com

.

an article by Trennis Henderson, entitled, "Jim Henry urges Pastors, Deacons to Pursue Unity in Christ," he states, "What holds us together is prayer, the first element of unity."[33]

Church Meeting Diverse Needs

Today's church is not only a gathering place for worship, but it truly has become the hospital and delivery room for those experiencing life at its fullness and for those who are struggling in every aspect of it. It is for these reasons that the deacons at SJBC must be better prepared to serve the diverse congregation frequenting the church's doors daily. Very few models have extensively planned programs of study for the deacon. Much research simply figures on the qualifications and role responsibilities of the ministry; however, the ability to continue growing within the servants' office is often forsaken or not as researched and developed. It is about a "fair balance or a distributive justice, in which God's family all get an equitable share of God's world."[34]

Jesus, throughout His ministry, taught the disciples at every teachable moment. From the Model Prayer to actually modeling ministry for the disciples, Jesus made His lessons come alive for all who witnessed it. His disciples had to know about, not only prayer, but also how to lay hands on the sick and how to minister to the least of these my brethren. Those in the deacon ministry could not just be simply believers in Jesus. Their very selection by Jesus placed them at a higher level in the ministry, yielding greater works that was to be done.[35] This higher call warranted a higher commitment, unlike

---

[33] Trennis Henderson, Editor of Western Recorder, *News Journal of the Kentucky Baptist Convention,* accessed April 7, 2015.

[34] Borg and Crossan, 224.

[35] A.B. Bruce, *The Training of the Twelve* (ReadaClassic.com: USA, 2010), 15.

other previous responses generated. Jesus took time with His disciples, admonishing

them as they grew in wisdom and stature, just as He did in the Luke 2:52 account. [36] Not

only did Jesus grow under His Father's tutelage, but He also found favor with people.

Those, who have been called out for such service, must be humble enough to receive

instruction. Leaders, as part of the deacon ministry, have to exercise enough faith to walk

on water. That type of radical faith could only come through attempting to apply all they

had been taught. Though sometimes unsure, they had to "do it afraid," just as Joyce

Meyers advocates. [37] Deacons, as leaders in the church with their human frailties, have to

spend quality time in the Word, teaching, as well as being taught. God expects His

leaders to use whatever He has given them to accomplish the Master's purpose. [38]

Parallel to this notion is that every training program or model for the deacon must be

infused with the fruit of the spirit, as in Galatians 5:22-23. [39] Growth and maturity in the

Word cannot be developed without these spiritual qualities operating in the life of the

believer. Once the deacon member decides to please God more than anyone else, he then

is ready to receive from others only what is helpful and move on to the next phase of

realizing his calling from God. [40]

Literature suggests the deacon leaders, regardless of the training model employed,

must become interdependent on each other as they assist in performing the pastor's

---

[36] Luke 2:52.

[37] Joyce Meyers, *Do It Afraid!:Obeying God in the Face of Fear* (New York: FaithWords, 2008), 30.

[38] Wagner, 55.

[39] Galatians 5:22.

[40] Bruce Wilkinson, *The Dream Giver* (Sisters, OR: Multnomah Publishing Co, 2003), 107.

sacerdotal duties. It is when the deacon experiences a relationship with God that God promote him to go higher and deeper. That height and depth is only for those yielded vessels that choose to accept the invitational call to service. They are willing to be taught. They are apt to teach. They are willing to receive 'holy stretch marks' in and through their walk. Deacon leaders must be lifelong learners. Learning the Lord's Prayer as a child was only the beginning to establishing a model for instruction. Yet, when a leader has been set aside for special and specific ministry, then it becomes essential that they accept the responsibility to learn everything they can, as often as they can. To achieve the full benefits of training of any kind, the deacon member, both individually and collectively, must have specific goals that will benefit the deacon and the overall ministry.[41]

It is a privilege to serve God. Jesus told His disciples in Luke 17:10, "When you have done all those things which you are commanded, you can say we are unprofitable servants. We have done what was our duty to do."[42] Serving in leadership allows one to exercise their earthly assignment. Jesus, allowing the deacon to serve, suggests His gratitude for their obedience. The deacon must be one of the first to abide in Christ Jesus and when He comes back, we may have confidence and not be ashamed before Him at His coming.[43] That confidence suggests a prepared, trained leader ready for service. The deacon leader, regardless of the model under which they are trained, bases their

---

[41] Gary C. Newton, *Growing Towards Spiritual Maturity* (Wheaton, IL: Crossway Books, 2004), 109.

[42] Luke 17:10.

[43] 1 John 2:28.

expectation of reward in visible proof.[44] As a servant leader, one may rarely see the fruit of their labor. However, they must still serve. Our posture for learning directly correlates with our quality of service. The deacon ministry, under the pastor's tutelage, is to equip God's people to do His work and build up the church, the body of Christ.

Pivotal Disciplines for Deacon Training

Knowledge of the scripture and meaningful ways to put it in action are two of the pivotal disciplines inherent in deacon education. Mental health issues sitting in the pew require a basic knowledge; however, the deacon must know when to make necessary referrals with permission from the pastor. This epitomizes collaboration at its best. Using models such as those previously discussed will "allow church leaders to work with other entities and social orders to meet the needs of the community"[45]. Involving other appropriate resources and/or agencies was germane to the training process.

Comparison and Contrast

The previously reviewed models have re-training at its core. Malphurs' Model, suggesting inclusion of more intrinsic values, is celebratory. The application of knowledge of the scriptures inherent in the Ebenezer, Shalom and Love and Faith models are not only foundational, but also pervasive throughout the model's implementation. The model the researcher promotes has education at its core, but suggests a more structured, three-year planned program of study that is relevant and based on scriptures. Regardless of when one becomes a part of the deacon ministry, they will be able to enter the training series without significant pause.

---

[44] Wilkinson, *A Life God Rewards*, 109.

[45] Brochure on Collaborative Leadership, *United Theological Seminary*, 2003, accessed February 13, 2015 http://united.edu/collaborativeleadership.

This model recognizes where each deacon is on their spiritual walk and builds from that point. The model provides training for all needs. This is the same mindset used when serving the membership. There are basic assumptions inferred in this model's design and organization. Assumptions are that anyone in the deacon ministry has far more than basic knowledge of the scriptures. The researcher believes they all have met the 1 Timothy 3 qualifications and have been proven of their knowledge of the scriptures through their walk, example and active participation of serving within the ministry. They have evolved as leaders after God's own heart. Just as important, they reflect the heart of the pastor who reflects the heart of Christ. "Our Lord was willing to get his hands dirty and bloody to show us what a true leader looks like."[46]

The researcher seeks to have the model as an exemplar of effective 21st century deacon ministry. Ebenezer Baptist, Shalom and Love and Faith models provide strong foundations for the researcher's model. These models are firmly tied with scripture. "Jesus invoked the final stage only after systematic teachings, tutelage and empowerment and thus they were better able to be selected for servant leadership, better enabling them to touch and empower the lives of others,"[47] according to Dr. James Taylor. The researcher's model uses all of these values, but incorporates a more systematic way for the deacon to train and serve as an extension of the pastor's arms over a multi-year planned timeframe.

---

[46] Kevin Harney, "Leadership from the Inside Out," Zondervan, 2007, Grand Rapids, MI, 122.

[47] Taylor, 25.

CHAPTER III

THEORETICAL FOUNDATIONS

Theoretical Foundations

The theoretical foundations behind creating a collaborative approach to

deacon/pastor ministry at SJBC, begins with my agreement with Kate Ward-Turner:

> One of the most important decisions contemporary churches face is the
> development of deacons and the improvement of the deacons' ministry, while the
> whole church is obligated to make sure that deacons are trained for the deacon
> ministry, the responsibility for their training rest primarily with the pastor. No
> undertaking by the pastor is more imperative. No other pursuit will pay any
> greater dividends to the pastor, the deacons
> and the church.[1]

These sentiments and language are so accurate, even within the urban context of

the researcher's current ministry. His current experiences are not surprising neither are

they contextual only in this urban faith community, but they are the same contextual

experiences observed and practiced within the rural faith communities of the Eastern

Shore of Virginia.

The need for a collaborative approach to deacon/pastor ministry is based on the

experiences and challenges that had occurred during the researcher's current assignment

at the SJBC. Through prayer, the researcher discerned in this present faith

community, the deacons of the church needed persistent Biblical teaching on leadership

and organizational structure that is consistent with the Word of God. There had to be a

pedagogy for learning that would be easy for them to comprehend. The Word of God is

clear to us in the book of Hosea, *"My people are destroyed from lack of*

---

[1] Kate Ward-Turner, 35.

knowledge. "[2] The people were destroyed, not from lack of knowledge in general, but from failing to know – that is to take to heart and follow the law of God. Without the guidance of God's law, people will lose their way, stumble and go astray, which would have caused Israel to be estranged from God. Persons who serve or desire to serve as officers or ministry leaders must be discipled, taught, and motivated to spiritual maturity. As their pastor and spiritual leader, I must consistently keep them in a learning posture as Jesus did with his disciples; even Jesus himself was to be instructed by his father. Luke records, *"And Jesus grew in wisdom and stature, and in favor with God and men."*[3]

Norman Shawchuck and Roger Heuser in their book, *Leading the Congregation-Caring for Yourself While Serving the People,* made many profound statements. Herein lays the heart beat and backbone of spirituality for Christian ministry. As we consider the substance of Jesus' spirituality, constantly ask yourself this question, "If Jesus, being the Son of God, felt He needed to adhere to the means of grace in order to sustain his ministry, can we possibly hope to respond fully to our call without living within these means?"[4]

Believers of God who make up our today's church should be receptive to teaching and preaching. We must be teachable by those who are experienced and who have been properly educated through the various opportunities offered such as conferences, workshops, local ministry associations and Bible studies. It is imperative to know that

---

[2] Hosea 4:6.

[3] Luke 2:52.

[4] Roger Heuser and Norman Shawchuck, *Leading the Congregation: Caring for Yourself While Serving Others* (Nashville, TN: Abington Press 1993), Kindle eBbook.

the Lord, who saved us, wants us to have favor with his father and with men. This reveals that a vertical relationship with God is necessary in order to have a horizontal relationship with our fellow man. It is a perfect picture of what the cross represents. We must adopt this concept in the today's church and the church at large if we are going to gain the favor of our communities and add to our number daily those who will be saved.

Finally, a leader must display the relational skills to mobilize people. Without favor, a person may still fail to take anyone with them to the goal. A leader has a compass in their head and a magnet in their heart. Some of the concepts a leader must embrace are as follows:

1. Communication-Leaders must develop listening skills and the ability to share ideas convincingly.

2. Motivation-Leaders must mobilize others for mutual benefit and empowerment.

3. Delegation-Leaders must share their authority, responsibility and ownership of the vision.

4. Confrontation-Leaders must have backbone and be able to resolve relational differences.

5. Reproduction-Leaders must be able to equip and train a team of people to accomplish the goal.[5]

---

[5] Ron McManus, "Four Qualities of Effective Leadership: Participant Note Sheet. *iTeen Challenge,* accessed March 14, 2015 http://www.iteenchallengetraining.org/uploads/FOUR_Qualities_of_Leadership2.ppt.

It is these qualities that must be developed in today's leaders regardless of the gender or age of those who choose to be a servant leader within the Gospel ministry. We must re-envision the way pastors allow persons to serve on ministries, particularly where they are elected and/or chosen based on kinship, friendship or other threatening associations and allowed to serve with no knowledge of the position or accountability to it. This will cause the whole body to be ineffective during a time when we really need the church to be effective.

"A Partnership of Similar Hearts: A Collaborative Approach to Deacon/Pastor Ministry at St. James Baptist Church" will be an ongoing process of developing persons within the congregation to serve as servant leaders in the ministerial context, such as deacon. This attempt will be done through Biblical teaching on the relevance of service and discipleship as prerequisites. Aubrey Malphurs states that "A Christian leader is a Christian. At the very core of the Christian leader's life is his or her personal conversion. To be a Christian leader, one must first be a Christian. This is the starting place for all Christians in leadership."[6] This is the essence of who we are first and foremost. This model includes, but not limited to training on Christian doctrine, biblical and current role of the deacon, conflict resolution and crisis management. The foundations for these are modeled in the scriptures that we will explore in this chapter.

Old Testament Training Models of Partnership and Collaboration Among Servant Leaders

A strong reality of productive partnership and collaboration among servant leaders is that two can accomplish more than one, and a team can accomplish more than

[6] Malphurs,15.

an individual. Solomon speaks to this in Ecclesiastes 4:9-10. "Two are better than one, because they have a good return for their labor; if either of them falls down, one can help the other up. But pity anyone who falls and has no one to help them up."[7] The researcher is in agreement with Dr. John Maxwell, who in his book *The 17 Indisputable Laws of Teamwork*, uses the acronym T E A M – Together, Everyone, Achieves, More Ministry, to further emphasize the need for this type of collaboration.[8] In the Old Testament Pastor Moses give two models for collaboration among servant leaders. In Exodus 18:13-26 we find pastor Moses being looked upon as the judge over disputes, complaints, and matters of interpretation for the nation of Israel. Moses was ministering to the people from morning to evening.[9] Day after day this activity became a massive burden. Moses' father-in-law Jethro recognized the level of increasing fatigue and burden on Moses and offered Godly counsel to select men that could share this burden. These were to be able men that fear God, men of truth, hating covetousness, and men who could be placed to rule over hundreds or thousands of people. Moses would teach them what the judgments and statues of God were so these servant leaders might minister to the people in the small matters. Pastor Moses would still manage the greater matters of the people. Archie Luper in his article *"The Jethro Principle"* says "Managers do things right, but leaders do the right thing."[10] Because the man of God put the needs of

---

[7] Ecclesiastes 4:9-10 King James Version (KJV).

[8] John Maxwell, *The 17 Indisputable Laws of Team Work* (Nashville, TN; Thomas Nelson Publishers, 2013).

[9] Exodus 18:13-26 (NIV).

[10] Archie Luper, "The Jethro Principle," *FaithSite.com*, accessed March 14, 2015 http://cbti.faithsite.com.

the people of God ahead of his pride, and the need for partnership and collaboration in the proper priority the people are blessed with peace and ministry continues to grow.[11]

The Book of Numbers presents to us a life experience reality that every committed pastor has experienced in his or her pastoral leadership role as they lead God's people to the destination given to them in vision. Approximately 40 years after the exodus from Egypt, the Israelites were now preparing to enter the land of Canaan. God had supernaturally enabled Pastor Moses to lead them through those challenging events, occurrences and some re-occurrences. These challenges may have opposed their journey as a nation who was anticipating the new. All of these questions among the nation escalated into murmurings against Moses and God. Numbers 11:1 states, "Now the people complained about their hardships in the hearing of the Lord, and when He heard them, His anger was aroused."[12]

The constant and daily hearing of this murmuring posture from God's own elected Israel had become such a burden on Moses, but this great burden was not to be Moses' burden alone, but more so the God who has given him this great task.

> The Lord said to Moses brings me seventy of Israel's elders who are known to you as leaders and officials among the people. Have them come to the tent of meeting that they may stand there with you. I will come down and speak with you there, and I will take of the spirit that is on you and put the spirit on them. They will help you carry the burden of the people so that you will not have to carry it alone."[13]

Obviously, Moses had received instructions from the Lord on who to choose as leaders among the people (70 elders) that He may place the burden of Moses ministry upon them.

---

[11] David Jeremiah, *The Jeremiah Study Bible NKJV* (Brentwood, TN; Worthy Publishing, 2013).

[12] Numbers 11:1.

[13] Numbers 11:16-17.

This act of God served as an endorsement that Moses' provocation led to the appointment of these seventy men to assist him in the administration issues of the camp. Moses will no longer have to carry this burden alone, but will now be able to reduce his attempt to meet the needs of a vast population by himself This oneness seemed to symbolize three characteristics needed to equip Moses. First, it symbolizes physical support. God was supplying Moses with the physical help that he needed to assist him in meeting the physical needs of the people as they would journey into a new land and future.

> That's the way the church and ministers must function. The minister cannot deal with every little thing; he needs some physical help, some physical support to deal with the things of lesser importance so he can be freed to handle more pressing matters. That support must come from those who have committed themselves to share as partners with their spiritual leader in the ministry to which the Lord has called him.[14]

These servant leaders must come from among the people to be tangibly and visibly present, so that they may be verbally instructed on how the matters at hand will be executed. It is also significant that these appointed leaders be physically present and accessible so that those whom they will be serving will know who they are.

Second, it symbolizes an equal compassion between the pastor and leader for the ministry of serving and meeting the needs of God's people. Scripture tells us in Amos 3:3 "How can two walk together lest they be agreed"[15]. Pastor and those chosen among the people to their church leader must have a compassion of oneness that burns within both persons. This component of oneness (partnership) creates a cohesiveness that is necessary in meeting the demands, as well as the vision and mission for today's

---

[14] Robyn Gool, *Proper Attitudes Toward Leadership* (Tulsa, Oklahoma: Christian Publishing Services, Inc, 1987), 119.

[15] Amos 3:3.

church. This display of moral conduct in Moses' appointed elders (servant leaders) not only allowed them to display the spirit of God, but also the spirit of their leader Moses. This is the authentication of a shared compassion.

Third, it symbolizes the necessity to be spiritually empowered. If there is going to be a oneness, accountability, and productivity in accomplishing God's will for His people, there must be a supernatural empowerment that occurs in both pastor and appointed servant leaders. Moses was advised to select men who were already known as elders because of their wisdom, conduct, and ministry to others.[16] They were to be men who had a relationship with God. Moses created an atmosphere of collaboration with prayer and teaching them the Law of God.[17] Our cognitive ingenuity and physical efforts are insufficient as it renders us powerless to perform such spiritual tasks that are at hand. God gave to Moses those who are now capable of not only supporting him, but who are also ready to function in assisting him in their office. This new binary relationship that is now initiated and shared by all the stakeholders will now allow the elders to be sensitive to Moses heart as well as the governing needs of the people (Israel). All of Moses' sensitivities, frustrations, passions and burdens are solidified in all of their hearts now. This is not to discredit the elders by saying that they may not have had these qualities. However, it is certain that now we know by the evidence of their ability to work together that they were spiritually endowed and active in their newly appointed role of servant leadership. This Old Testament paradigm gives us a true model of how to resolve some of today's church issues, and addresses the needs of the pastor and leaders

---

[16] David Guzik, "Commentary on Numbers 15:1", accessed November 13, 2014 http://www.studylight.org/commentaries/guz/view.cgl?book=nu&chapter=015. 1997-2003.

[17] Ibid.

by initiating a spirit of partnership and collaboration. Both the leadership and congregation can now effectively and efficiently fulfill the kingdom's agenda with a shared responsibility of oneness.

Pastor Moses was worn out, depressed, exhausted and was ready to give up. Hearing his cry, God answered and gave him what he needed. This should be the prayer of every leader, which is to hear from God and to receive instructions as well as the physical help needed to administrate the vision given by God. The members of the deacon ministry must bear the burden of the people with the pastor and have the pastor's spirit. They must share the pastor's passion, caring for God's people.

New Testament Training Models for Partnership and Collaboration Among Servant Leaders

The Book of Acts distinguishes deacons as problem-solvers of church problems. Using Acts 6, Dr. Luke presents to his readers two problems in the Jerusalem church. One was a good problem, substantial church growth. The second, not so good, was the murmuring or complaining among the people. "In those days when the number of disciples was increasing, the Hellenistic Jews (Greeks) among them complained against the Hebraic Jews (Hebrews) because their widows were being overlooked in the daily distribution of food."[18] Luke's writing suggests that the growth and the complaining were happening simultaneously, and the complaint was caused by the neglect that was identified about this time. Acts 4:4 references 5000 men added to the church not including women and children[19]. The needs of the people soon overwhelmed the existing

---

[18] Acts 6:1.

[19] Acts 4:4.

structures and resources of the early church. New Christians from all different places, with different languages, different views, different politics, and different walks of life, were now a part of the church. "Now there was in Jerusalem God-fearing Jews from every nation under heaven"[20]. The apostles assessed the murmuring and complaining and involved the congregation in seeking a favorable solution by admonishing them, "It is not desirable that we should leave the word of God and serve tables. Therefore brethren, seek out from among you seven men of good reputation, full of the Holy Spirit and wisdom, whom we may appoint over this business."[21]

Luke allows us to gain additional insight into the role of these servants (deacons) with the dissection of the two groups of widows. Acts 6:1 identifies two groups of widows in the Jerusalem church, the Hellenists Jews and the Hebraic Jews. The complaint was that the Greeks were being dealt with unfairly in the daily distribution of the welfare to the widows. Some argued that this problem was because of a language problem. John R. Stott adds "It was more than a language issue; it was cultural issues that caused these two groups to remain in tension despite the unifying death of Jesus Christ for all of them"[22]. They were left to feel neglected. The neglected members of today's church may include single mothers, the homeless, and Generation X. Jennifer Maggie reports that 67% of single mothers do not actively attend church because they don't feel they belong in the house of God. They fear they will be judged and that no one

---

[20] Acts 2:5.

[21] Acts 6:2-3.

[22] John Stott, *The Message of Acts* (Downers Grove. IL: Inter-Varsity, 1991), 56.

is concerned or understands their journey.[23] There was natural suspicion between the two groups, and Satan tried to take advantage of the situation by creating a conflict. As instructed by the apostles, the disciples sought out seven men of good reputation, full of the Holy Spirit and wisdom, and the apostles appointed them over "this business". These men were selected as a solution to the problem of certain members, and certain cultures being neglected. They were also used to prevent any further schism and disputes in the church. They were instrumental in making sure the ministry of the Word of God through the apostles was not hindered. God could have chosen any number of different scenarios to solve these issues, but he chose to give us a deacon model as part of the solution equation. Acts 6 and 1 Timothy: 3 gives us the biblical qualifications for these servants (deacons). "Wherefore, brethren, look ye out among you seven men of honest report, full of the Holy Ghost and wisdom, whom we may appoint over this business."[24]

We find recorded in 1 Timothy 3:8-10, "Likewise must the deacons be grave, not double-tongued, not given to much wine, not greedy of filthy lucre; holding the mystery of the faith in a pure conscience. And let these also first be proved; then let them use the office of a deacon, being found blameless."[25] The gravity of the admonition from the apostles to the disciples dictates the importance this servant position. Naylor asks "Since the work of the deacon is so vital, what kinds of men are adequate for it? Obviously not just anybody will do, for a church is a spiritual concern. Spiritual qualifications are basic,

---

[23] Jennifer Maggio, Five Reasons Churches should serve Single moms. *Pastors.com,* May 17, 2012, accessed March 14, 2015. www.pastors.com/5-reasons-your-church-should-serve-single-moms.

[24] Acts 6:3 KJV.

[25] 1 Timothy 3:8-10 KJV.

and many present problems have come about from ignoring this."[26] In response to this question, Luke suggests in Act 6 that the deacon must be a saved man. The church was instructed to "look ye out among you". The deacons were to be active members of the community of faith. Spiritual fruit should be observable. Thomas Watson describes observable fruit as follows: Inward Fruit is love, joy, peace, patience, gentleness, goodness and faith. Outward Fruit is having good speech and good works, and Kindly Fruit is being holy in our calling and relationships."[27] The "walk" should speak louder than the "talk".

The deacon must be "of honest report" (Acts 6) or reverent (1Timothy 3:8). This means the deacon has a good name among the people, be trusted with money and with confidential information and worthy of respect. As indicated by Dr. Robert Naylor, the deacon must be a spiritual person, "full of the Holy Ghost"[28]. The word "full" means thoroughly permeated with[29]. It is this filling that allows the Holy Ghost boldness to witness for the Lord. Deacons are also controlled and led by wisdom and the Spirit of God. This is a person whom does not allow his judgment to be clouded by emotion or personal opinion.

The deacon must not be double-tongued. 1 Timothy 3:8 could be referring to either a gossiping person or one that says one thing and does another.[30]. Lee and Griffin

---

[26] Robert E. Naylor, *The Baptist Deacon*, (Nashville, TN: Broadman and Holman Publishers, 1955), 14.

[27] Thomas Watson, "Trees of Righteousness," Grace Gems, accessed March 18, 2015 http://www.gracegems.org/watson/trees_of_righteousness.htm.

[28] Naylor, 15.

[29] Ibid., 17.

[30] Timothy 3:8 King James Version (KJV).

in 1 and 2 Timothy Titus commentary suggest the deacon is not to be *dilogos,* meaning not to spread rumors to different groups of listeners. [31] The deacon's word must be dependable. [32] Drunkenness or other forms of substance abuse cannot be part of the deacon's repertoire. The Holy Spirit provides the controls for all deacons, not chemicals.

Deacons frequently go from house to house setting proper examples and upholding standards. Avarice of any sort, especially money, does not figure into the deacon's equation. The biblical phrase here has to do with "not making a dishonest dollar" but maintaining a spiritual attitude toward money. The deacon is charged with the requirement of "holding the mystery of the faith" with a pure conscience. They must know the doctrines of faith so that they stand against error. The deacon must then have a behavior that is consistent with his beliefs. First Timothy 3:10 suggests that another qualification for a deacon is to be "tested" or proven. [33] This term implies that the deacon's qualifications to serve must be authenticated using ongoing testing and examination by the church. The deacon must be blameless and above reproach (*anegkletos*), meaning without charge or accusation. [34] Deacons extend the ministry of those preaching the Word; therefore their lives should not be a liability to the kingdom, nor draw attention from people receiving the Word of God. Their lives should be an asset to the people of whom they serve as well as to the pastor.

---

[31] Thomas D. Lea and Hayne P. Griffin, Jr., *The New American Commentary 1, 2 Timothy, Titus* Volume 34 accessed November 14, 2014 www.olivetree.com/store/product.php?productid=17914.

[32] Ibid.

[33] 1 Timothy 3:10 KJV.

[34] *The New Testament Greek Lexicon Bible Dictionary,* s.v. "blameless," accessed March 14, 2015, http://www.biblestudytools.com/lexicons/greek (accessed January 6, 2015).

As this congregation grows in numbers and experiences spiritual growth, the needs of the congregation are becoming more diverse. The demands on the pastor for proper administration, prayer, preaching, and intense study are constantly evolving, and never ending. The researcher is finding, however, that the mindset and training of the current deacons will need to be updated to address the current challenges of today's church. The current perception that the previous way of training and doing is adequate will have to be transformed to model what is purposeful for today's church. If a collaborative partnership is to be established and functional, training of servant leaders must be consistent, biblical and at times out-of-the-box. Dr. Gary L. McIntosh talks about the life cycles of the church.[35] He analyzes the church from the initial "emerging" stage, powered by vision and commitment, to the "dying" stage when the building is empty and only the memories of "how thing used to be" remains. Dr. McIntosh emphasizes that to prevent or stop the destructive forces, plot a forward focus, and keep the church's mission at the forefront; there must be a paradigm shift in thinking and teaching, to change the method of ministry, not the mission.[36] He states that churches grow and then plateau. It is sometimes easy to rest on the laurels and traditions of the past plateau to move the body of Christ to the next level. With these issues in mind, the researcher will seek to develop a training model that helps to move the deacons of SJBC from resting not only on the traditions of the past, but to help usher in an atmosphere of collaboration between pastor and deacons and embrace effective training and leadership for the paradigm of today's church.

---

[35] Gary L. McIntosh, *Taking Your Church to the Next Level-What Got You Here Won't Get Your There*, (Grand Rapids, MI: Baker Books, 2009), 12-17.

[36] McIntosh, 59.

Role of the Deacon

Three primary Greek words are used to describe our English word deacon. One is *Diakoneo* which means "to be an attendant, to minister to one, to wait upon."[37] In the New Testament it refers to waiting on someone at a table as a waiter (Luke 22:24-27), helping or supporting someone (Matthew 25:24). Jesus gives us an illuminated look at service and ministry in Mark 10:45 which states "For even the Son of man came not to be ministered unto, but to minister, and to give his life a ransom for many."[38] Jesus reminds us that genuine ministry is done for the benefit of those we minister too, not to benefit the one ministering.[39] In Luke 8:3 Joanna and Susanne give us additional examples of ministering from the heart for the benefit of others.[40] In this role, the deacon ministers in a way to improve the lives of all the congregants he/she serves.

The second word for describing deacons is *Diakonia* which means "service or attendance as a servant".[41] It refers to all manners of service in the New Testament. Acts 11:29 provides a picture of the role of the servant leader in the distribution of alms and giving to the poor. Deacons are often needed to serve a specific ministry in the Body of Christ. Romans 12:7 encourages the deacon to minister in his/her gifting with grace. In 2 Corinthians 8:3-4 we find the role of service ministry as resources are provided for meeting basic needs by monetary and spiritual means. In today's church, the deacon who

---

[37] *The New Testament Greek Lexicon Bible Dictionary.*

[38] Mark 10:45.

[39] Cambridge Greek New Testament for School and Colleges, *Study Light*, accessed January 8, 2015 http://www.studylight.org.commentarys/cgt/view.cgl.

[40] Luke 8:3.

[41] *The New Testament Greek Lexicon Bible Dictionary.*

serves in these roles provides active service to meet a specific need, and does it with a willing attitude. Deacons paint a picture of spirit empowered service that is guided by their faith in God.

The third Greek word for describing deacons is *Diakonos* which suggests "a waiter, attendant", "servant or minister"[42]. It refers to a helper or encourager in scripture. Romans 16:1 introduce Phoebe as a servant (diakonos) of the church, and her ministries of service. Paul here lets us know that women had important roles in the early church and in today's church. (Life Application Bible – KJV. Tyndale House Publishers Inc. Wheaton, Illinois.10/2011) Philippians 1:1 uses diakonos as an official of the church, or recognized position of service. We are also given an example of this role as Timothy is sent to encourage and serve the Thessalonians in 1 Thessalonians 3:2.

The role of the deacon in today's church often calls for them to be a minister of encouragement. Just as Timothy was used to minister to the Thessalonians, the deacon in today's church creates a proper atmosphere for service by showing love to all of God's creations. He is then able to minister the kindness of encourager. The Greek word, *Dioko,* is the root word from which the other three are derived. It means "to run or hasten on errands"[43] (King James Version New Testament Greek Lexicon). The image here, "*to kick up dust*", is of a servant working so hard and moving so fast that he leaves a cloud of dust in his path.

Each of these biblical interpretations denotes a servant that is of service to others. The researcher is in agreement with William T. Ditewig's claim, "The

---

[42] Ibid.

[43] Ibid.

Christological dimension of deacon is expressive of the Kenosis of God. Christ own

Kenosis is of course a part of each Christian life, and of the life of the Christian

community."[44] Ditewig further expands on Jean Corbon who speaks of two kenoses of

the spirit. The gift to us of God's ever faithful love must be answered by an authentic life

of charity which the Holy Spirit pours into our hearts. We too must give our gift fully;

that is, we must divest ourselves in that same Kenosis of love.[45]

Servant-hood

"A Partnership of Similar Hearts: A Collaborative Approach to Deacon/Pastor

Ministry at St. James Baptist Church" is a clear illumination of the light that shined

through the servant-hood of our Lord Jesus. Philippians chapter two, verses five through

eight states:

> Your attitude should be the same as that of Christ Jesus. Who, being in very
> nature God, did not consider equality with God something to be grasped, but
> made himself nothing, taking the very nature of a servant, being made in human
> likeness. And being found in appearance as a man, he humbled himself and
> became obedient to death – even death on a cross.[46]

True and authentic partnership begins with servant-hood. Jesus, who is our Lord, in

whom the foundation of the church is founded and built, is the epitome of love and

servant-hood. Servant-hood is the fruit of a transformed life by the works of the Holy

Spirit in the life of the believer. "For even the Son of Man came to serve, and not to be

served."[47] The theology of a deacon must be examined under the light of servant-

---

[44] William T. Ditewig, *The Emerging Diaconate* (Mahwah, NJ: Paulist Press, 2007), 130.

[45] Ibid., 130.

[46] Philippians 2:5-8.

[47] Matthew 20:28.

hood: servant-hood to God, servant-hood under the pastor, and servant-hood to the faith community.

The first century church serves as a precursor to today's church, just as the Israelites in the Old Testament serves as a precursor to the first century church. The experiences of Moses with the Israelites gives us a clear window into the early church of the New Testament wherein these two communities of faith were distinct in their cultural context, they both shared the commonality of community complaint, and contention within. In both biblical parallels God did not leave Moses or the apostles to their own cognitive solutions. Instead He initiated a solution that would serve as a dual attempt to preserve His kingdom.

God wanted to exemplify His love by meeting the physical, spiritual and cultural needs of the early church. Philippians 4:19(NIV) says, "My God shall supply all your needs according to the riches of His glory in Christ Jesus."[48] Psalm 84:11 adds "No good thing will be withheld from them that walk uprightly."[49] This love provided an Old and a New Testament model to help prevent the church from majoring in its minors, and to focus on its purpose, to make disciples. Matthew 28:19-20(NIV) says, "Therefore go and make disciples of all nations, baptizing them in the name of the father and of the son and of the Holy Spirit, and teaching them to obey everything I have commanded you. And surely I am with you always, to the very end of the age."[50]

---

[48] Philippians 4:19 NIV.

[49] Psalm 84:11.

[50] Matthew 28:19.

Today's pastor, like the Old Testament leaders and New Testament apostles, has increasing challenges, some external, but mostly internal. There are generational challenges, apathy problems, leadership development challenges, evangelism challenges, and time constraints that become more and more demanding. Simmons proposed that our churches are victims of rapid increase in moral bankruptcy and dysfunctional relationships.[51] The institution of family was once considered a sacred and safe entity but has now been downgraded to a blend of options and lifestyles. Our communities are ravaged with insatiable appetites for money, sex and power. Just as God provided the needs for the nations of the Old Testament and the church of the New Testament with servants and assistants, He has provided today's pastor with a servant leader (deacon) to share the burden of the pastor, protect the pastor, pray with and for the pastor, and stay in touch with the ever changing needs of the church.

In conclusion, the researcher agrees with Rev. Margaret Minnicks, who in her workshop for Deacons and the Women's Auxiliary at First Shiloh Baptist Church in Mechanicsville, Virginia states "Paul says in 1 Corinthians 9:20-23, in order to share the gospel message so people can come to Christ, we need to be on common ground with them. We can do this by always keeping the same message of Jesus Christ, but we must change the method of how we share.[52] Sharing the message of Jesus Christ requires the partnership and collaboration of servant leaders with the pastor so that no one is omitted from being ministered. God has given us biblical models to demonstrate what service and ministering looks like regardless of gender, position, or title. The biblical models

---

[51] Simmons, 2015.

[52] Margaret Minnicks, "Changing the Method, Not the Message," October 2012 accessed April 13, 2015 http://www.examiner.com/article/minister-facilitated-the-workshop-changing-the-method-not-the-message.

also show us the need for sensitivity of the servant leader to the pastor's spirit, and the pastor's passion for all people. The biblical models emphasized the need for encouragement of the deacon and the pastor. Jesus himself reminds us that the Son of God came to serve.

Paul teaches the importance of collaboration among co-laborers and servant leaders. It is this spirit of a collaborative approach to ministry that produces excellence in all areas of ministry. When asked by our deacons why is there such an urgency for partnership and collaboration? The researcher's response was and still is that souls are at stake, and spiritual destinies are in the balance. It is when the servant leaders and pastor takes on a collaborative approach together that the community of faith witnesses a partnership of similar hearts of the deacon/pastor ministry at St. James Baptist Church performing with excellence.

CHAPTER IV

GOING BEYOND THE TITLE

This chapter will outline the methodology used for training deacons for the collaboration needed with the pastor for such training. The title of this deacon training ministry model is "A Partnership of Similar Hearts: A Collaborative Approach to Deacon/Pastor Ministry at St. James Baptist Church." The context selected for this project was an examination of the deacons of SJBC in Greensboro, North Carolina. This church of approximately 800 members is found in an urban setting consisting of mostly African-American congregants. The key players for this ministry project included thirteen incumbent deacons and five newly appointed deacons who aspired from the ranks of the laity.

The researcher began his tenure at SJBC in prayer, study and almost a year of formal and informal observation of the entire congregation. From the findings came the hypothesis of this ministry model. It reflects two big ideas: 1) the deacons' lack of awareness in understanding the need for change from their traditional roles and responsibilities to meet the demands of the 21st century church; and 2) a lack of adequate training in the past within the deacon ministry's infrastructure to effectively serve the current congregation. Aubrey Malphurs, a leading expert on leadership issues, describes these inadequacies as a "leadership development crisis."[1] He further states that "We need a radical change to the typical 21st century pastor's church-leadership paradigm…Our churches need the mind-set of the military, which has made leadership development a

---

[1] Malphurs, 12.

part of their leaders' daily lives and an essential path to success."[2] Thus, the development of leaders, specifically the SJBC deacon, "must be the intentional process of helping established and emerging leaders at every level of ministry to assess and develop their Christian character and to acquire, reinforce, refine their ministry knowledge and skills."[3]

Objective

The objective of this project is to create a biblically-based deacon training model that is systematic in its design and implementation in order to transform its deacons to a level of servant leadership necessary to equip and empower. The product of this leadership development effort would also effectively and efficiently serve the people. Consequently, the premise is that by experiencing this deacon training model, the deacons will be equipped with the essential tools necessary for today's evolving ministry. These essential tools are the directed, yet practical lessons found in each module. Malphurs states that the "quality of leadership affects the quality of the ministry"[4]. Moreover, it serves to strengthen the bonds between the pastor, deacons, and the congregation, creating a partnership of similar hearts. This deacon training model consists of the following five modules:

1. SJBC Governance	2. Deacon Roles and Responsibilities
3. Spiritual Disciplines	4. Basic Ministry Skills
5. Deacon Partnership with the Pastor	

---

[2] Ibid.

[3] Malphurs, 23.

[4] Ibid.

The Planning Process

After almost a year in observation and getting to know the SJBC family, the researcher began to formulate his ideas on paper. Using both formal and informal measures from environmental scanning, he began to envision the initial steps for the training model. The researcher began to understand the church's culture, the way they had previously operated. That supposition was the gateway to understanding the strengths and challenges the church and its leadership had previously faced.

Through stakeholder interviews, observations, focus groups, surveys, and questionnaires the researcher began to assess and prioritize the specific needs of the deacons. It was apparent they lacked spiritual training and their ability to collaborate with the pastor and themselves was deficient. It became more evident that a systematic, planned program of training that included collaboration needed to be emphasized throughout the ministry. Previous efforts to train or re-train were sporadic and minimal at its best. The training model would be the first concerted effort to bridge and initiate this gap for the servant leaders. The researcher then looked for the best methods in gathering the needed information. It began with interviewing the current leadership. The initial deacon profile interviews consisted of the following questions:

1. How did you come to SJBC?

2. How long have you been a deacon?

3. What is your definition of a deacon?

4. What do you believe are your spiritual gifts?

5. What or how would you describe the mission of the church?

6. What would you like to see changed in the deacon ministry?

Research Method Selected

Although it goes without saying that this project will have some quantitative

measures, the majority of the research data will be qualitative. In the book *Qualitative*

Research Methods: A Data Collector's Field Guide, the writers established this

justification as a reason for using this method:

> The strength of qualitative research is its ability to provide complex textual
> descriptions of how people experience a given research issue. It provides
> information about the "human" side of an issue – that is, the often contradictory
> behaviors, beliefs, opinions, emotions, and relationships of individuals.
> Qualitative methods are also effective in identifying intangible factors, such as
> social norms, socioeconomic status, gender roles, ethnicity, and religion, whose
> role in the research issue may not be readily apparent. When used along with
> quantitative methods, qualitative research can help us to interpret and better
> understand the complex reality of a given situation and the implications of
> quantitative data.[5]

Once the decision was made as to what type of research to begin with, which was

qualitative data, the type of qualitative data sources to select was the next consideration.

Qualitative Data Sources

Prior to the determination of the qualitative measures, the researcher met with the

contextual associates that were selected after his installation. After permission was

obtained, a briefing was held to discuss their responsibilities and solicit their help in

administering the project. With the several qualitative data sources as a starting point for

---

[5]Natasha Mack, Cynthia Woodsong, Kathleen MacQueen, Greg Guest, Emily Namey, *Qualitative Research Methods: A Data Collector's Field Guide* (Research Triangle Park, NC: Family Health International) 2005.

the development of the Deacon Training Model, it provided a platform for the eventual implementation of this project (APPENDIX A).

The qualitative data sources used were informal and formal group interviews with key stakeholders, observations of social interactions of the membership specifically the deacons, a focus group, surveys and questionnaires. Below is a brief description of participants of each source with more detail added later in this project. The data collection sources are as follows:

- ***Stakeholder Interview Questions:*** Qualitative group interviews were initially conducted with the following stakeholders: 15 deacons and the 5 church staff (Office Manager, secretary, custodian and 2 musicians), associate ministers, the "Mother of the Church", members of the Pastoral Search committee and ministry presidents. In a joint session, the researcher asked questions of these stakeholders (APPENDIX H).

In a separate, less formal setting the researcher had meetings with the President of the High Point Educational and Missionary Baptist Association (HPEMBA), two other pastors who worked closely with SJBC when the church was without a pastor, and a city official who also was a member of the church. Contextual associates shared information with the researcher regarding three of the five models that would later be chosen to use for the project. The information shared regarding their model design was from Ebenezer Baptist Church, Love and Faith, and Shalom Ministries. The Malphurs and Orthodox Presbyterian Church models were also researched.

The process for measuring the outcomes were the compilation of the anecdotal data generated from the interviews. The researcher used this information to serve as part of the basis for developing the deacon training model. The group interviews lasted two hours, meeting twice within a six-week period, for approximately four hours of interaction. The researcher began to formulate the initial module areas that could become a part of the planned model. The initial module headings included the following: Deacon Roles, Specific Disciplines, Ministry Needs, Church Bylaws and Pastor Needs. Later in this document these modules will be redefined and renamed.

Observations: The researcher watched the dynamics and interactions of the entire congregation, especially the deacons' interactions with each other and with the laity. The research instrument used, observations, occurred while the researcher was in meetings, church services and other settings, including social ones. Deacon meetings, Sunday service, Church conference, and an afternoon church program will be cited later covering the interactions of the deacons and congregants. Though informal in nature, information gleaned from the observations would be used as another piece of data substantiating the need for training. The researcher measured the observation outcomes by determining trends and patterns inherent in the model's design. The observations occurred throughout the 2011-12 calendar year. The researcher could not adequately, nor reasonably estimate the number of observation opportunities or the actual number of persons observed.

Focus groups: The researcher used pre- and post-qualitative assessments with approximately ten deacons (APPENDIX I). The researcher determined the need for a collaborative deacon/pastor ministry at SJBC. The researcher wanted to hear directly from the deacons themselves. The focus groups were conducted over two Saturdays at the church, lasting 1.5 hours for the pre-assessment and 1.5 hours for the post-

assessment. Deacons were individually contacted and asked to participate in the focus

group while emphasizing that this was not a deacon meeting. They were told the purpose

and nature of the focus group. The researcher developed questions for the focus group

that would be beneficial for future training opportunities. It was believed that this would

be a great starting point for the development of a collaborative approach for a

deacon/pastor partnership. In the pre-assessment, conducted by the contextual associates

and the researcher, each deacon openly responded to each question, as they chose to. In

the post-assessment, each deacon privately wrote out their own response to the questions

asked. Answers appeared to be repetitive or influenced by responses from other deacons

during the pre-assessment. Resorting to a more personalized approach in the post-

assessment process allowed the deacons to individually, without influence, record their

own responses. What was created was a concise picture of their collective voices and

experiences while serving as deacons at SJBC. The Deacon's Roles and Responsibilities

Focus Group questions are listed in (APPENDIX K).

Surveys: The researcher surveyed the 18 deacons, 5 church staff members, 11 associate

ministers, and 19 deaconesses. The survey used was the 'To Deacon or Not to Deacon'

instrument (APPENDIX J). Each of the above stakeholders participated in the survey

sharing their individual perspective of the office of the deacon. The 30 minute survey was

conducted during a Leadership Retreat at Galilee Baptist Church, Winston-Salem, North

Carolina. Results from the compilation of this quantitative data will be reflected in

Chapter V. Outcomes measured will again become a part of the model to be designed

and implemented. In a separate setting, the Pastoral Search Committee informally shared with the researcher survey information on the status of the church. This information

consisted of specific characteristics the membership felt was needed in the SJBC

pastorate, in addition to the demographics of its membership.

Questionnaires: The researcher developed two questionnaires that were used to

interview the current deacons and another questionnaire that examined the current

deacons' understanding of their roles and responsibilities. The qualitative data consisted

of an analysis of the deacons' perception of their role responsibilities and how they

arrived at that conclusion. This additional data obtained, further identified the need to

establish a partnership of similar hearts in order to meet the needs of the deacons and

congregation. The questionnaire was administered December 2011. Forty-five minutes

was given for the completion of the questionnaire. The majority of the deacons present

utilized the entire time allotted with a few requiring an additional fifteen minutes.

Understanding the Church's Culture

Upon the researcher's arrival in May 2011 as pastor, SJBC had been without a

pastor for three years. The pastor was installed in October 2011. During the three-year

absence of a pastor, the church was led by the deacons. According to some congregants,

the church operations were fine, but it was apparent that some tensions still existed within

the church body. Some of the tensions that were created were couched in a belief by

some of the deacons holding a traditional paradigm of thinking, that deacons are the

"boss or the board in charge." Subsequently, opposing opinions with regards to handling

church issues increased. This resulted in a movement of SJBC as a church of honor for

its work in the community to a place of inner conflict and gossip, which tarnished its

longstanding reputation in the community. These challenges were no different from what was experienced in the early Christian church. Tom Hollinger, the founder of Leadership

Learning Initiatives, states:

> The early Christian church formed during a time of enormous change and
> tremendous pressure. To weather this onslaught, Jesus and his apostles selected,
> trained, and prepared successors to facilitate the spread of the gospel and ensure
> the church's survival. This Biblical model of succession planning played a vital
> role in providing development and continuity. Paul's epistles to Timothy and
> Titus provide particularly revealing attributes regarding the selection and
> development processes used by the early church for establishing and perpetuating
> competent, values-based leadership.[6]

Nonetheless, despite the challenges and conflicts that existed, it did bring about

awareness for re-training. This would better equip the deacons for servant leadership to

the congregation. However, it was critically important for the researcher to deal with the

lingering church hurt before any instruction for training could go forth or be of any effect.

First, the researcher sought the direction of the Lord in dealing with fractured

souls and bruised believers. Unifying both the deacon and the people was a priority.

Psalms 50:15 states, "Call upon me in the day of trouble".[7] Through prayer, fasting,

studying scriptures, and counseling from other pastors, particularly from the researcher's

Father in Ministry, these disciplines served as effective tools for resolving issues with

church hurt. Sermons, Bible Studies, deacon trainings, church-wide conferences and

prayer vigils covered love, forgiveness and healing. "Get rid of all bitterness, rage and

anger, brawling and slander, along with every form of malice. Be kind and

compassionate to one another, forgiving each other, just as in Christ God forgave you."[8]

This began the healing process; however, in no way did the researcher believe that this

---

[6] Tom Hollinger, "Leadership Development and Succession Planning: A Biblical Perspective for an Ethical Response" *Journal of Biblical Prospective in Leadership* 5 (2013): 157-164.

[7] Psalms 50:15.

[8] Ephesians 4:31-32.

would be the last time dealing with church conflict. Periodically, the researcher would teach more in depth on the healing process, attempting to be the purveyor of peace and unity.

Assessing and Prioritizing the Needs

Understanding the needs of the church leadership and requirements of the project, the researcher began with calling a special informational meeting with the deacons explaining the ministry project requirements and soliciting their help and support with the research. The researcher also discussed confidentiality and that ministry needs had been generated from observations and interviews. The researcher also shared information about pending training that would take place over the next 3 years. Issues and concerns were addressed in deacon meetings, Church-wide Leadership conferences and Deacon/Deacon-Elect trainings. Additionally, the researcher used information garnered from the focus groups using the pre- and post-assessments conducted at the church.

Selecting a Deacon Training Model

After reviewing several models, the deacon training format evolved. In this deacon training model, it is anticipated to transform the deacon ministry from foundational to now a very practical convergence of the discipline. Following throughout this chapter, training will address the deacon as servant leader and his service to a holy office.

Research Design, Measurement and Instrumentation

The researcher sought scholarly perspectives and biblical teachings to construct a Christ-centered ministry design to address specific areas of need for the SJBC deacon.

"For I always pray to the God of our Lord Jesus Christ, the Father of glory, that He may grant you a spirit of wisdom and revelation [of insight into mysteries and secrets] in the [deep and intimate] knowledge of Him."[9] The wisdom of the Lord helped to craft a unique deacon training model. The researcher first envisioned several overarching goals. In Habakkuk 2:2, the Word directs us, "And the LORD answered me, and said, write the vision, and make it plain upon tables, that he may run that readeth it."[10] The researcher's immediate goals for the SJBC deacon were to: 1) develop a Deacon Training Model, and 2) establish future Deacon Family Care Ministry Teams (APPENDIX L).

Ministry Program Design

The Deacon Training Model consisted of 5 modules over a 3 year period. Within each module are 3 or more biblically-based areas of training for the deacon ministry, and in some instances, for the laity at large. Infused throughout the modules are trainings that were conducive for the entire church body. Each training session lasted an average between 2-5 hours depending on the subject matter being taught and its targeted audience. The modules included: SJBC Governance, Deacon Roles and Responsibilities, Basic Ministry Skills, Spiritual Disciplines, and Deacon Partnership with the Pastor. The model also shows practical areas of application through ministry development with the allocation of appropriate resources. These trainings will begin the development of a Deacons Training Model and the future development of a Deacon Family Care Ministry. Below is a brief description of each module. Each session is held monthly, lasting two hours each. There are some sessions that may last longer. The flexibility in this model

---

[9] Ephesians 1:17.

[10] Habakkuk 2:2.

will allow for these type nuances. Occasional sessions may, depending on the purpose and audience, lasts up to eight hours, particularly the church-wide trainings. They usually begin on Friday evening from 7:00—9:00 and continue on Saturday, from 9:00 am—2:00 pm. Meals are often included.

Module 1: SJBC Governance assesses the deacon's understanding of the Vision and Mission statements of the church. An in-depth review and analysis of the church's bylaws, along with the ordinances of the church, articles of faith and the church covenant are critical pieces to understanding why we do church like we do. Recognizing the sanctity of baptism and communion, the researcher helped the deacons further understand the holiness associated with both ordinances. Deacons had to be at the forefront with the pastor to convey this singleness of heart (APPENDIX M 1).

Module 2: Deacon Roles and Responsibilities will establish an in-depth review of 1 Timothy 3 and Acts 6, discussing the Biblical Roles and Spiritual Qualifications and History of the Deacons. From various literatures, the researcher will review the Pastor as Shepherd, the Seven Shepherd Models and Deacon Characteristics which are intrinsic competencies in the module. While reviewing this module, essential focus will be on Women being an equal and integral part of a Deacon Ministry, unlike SJBC's current structure. Having an effective Deacon-Pastor relationship is what cements the quality of such a deacon training program (APPENDIX M 2).

Module 3: Spiritual Disciplines requires every leader to spend quality time with our Lord and Savior. Being able to fully submit to the Word of God, whether through Fasting, Bible Study or just Fellowship, are key to this faith walk. Every aspect of this module is undergirded and standing on the bank of prayer. Stewardship is a must while the church prepares for growth and harvest (APPENDIX M 3).

Module 4: Basic Ministry Skills promotes the need for all of the SJBC family to be active participants in church unity, knowing how to visit those hospitalized, those in crisis or even those situations where conflict may raise its head (APPENDIX M 4).

Module 5: Deacon Partnership with the Pastor is one of the most dynamic modules. It is imperative that the deacons serve as Aaron and Hur, as in Exodus 17, in holding the Man of God up while He ministers and serves. That godly partnership and understanding of his vision must be a center of everything deacons do while leading and serving (APPENDIX M 5).

Listed above are the modules which are inclusive of the research design, measurement and instrumentation of the SJBC Deacon Training Model. Data generated from the methodology will be reflected in Chapter V, Field Experience. This information will be reflected in the Appendices, and more clearly defined through the use of graphs and tables.

Sermons/Module Connection

The researcher selected the following five sermons as further support and documentation reflecting the modules specified. The five modules and sermons are:

Module	Sermon
Module 1: SJBC Governance	Crying over Spilled Milk
Module 2: Deacon Roles and Responsibilities	What the Word Will Do

Module 3: Spiritual Disciplines   Strength in the Journey

Module 4: Basic Ministry Skills   A Perfect Posture for Ministry

Module 5: Deacon Partnership with the Pastor   What Real Friends Do

Following is an overview of the sermons that the pastor connected with each module. The

sermon outlines will be reflected in the appendices (APPENDIX N).

Module 1 is SJBC Governance. The first sermon set the tone for the researcher's

introduction to the congregation at SJBC. In the message, "Crying Over Spilled Milk",

(APPENDIX N 1), the pastor used 1 Samuel 15:34-35 as the means to address where the

church was currently. The pastor began by defining the phrase, "crying over spilled

milk." The pastor reiterated that Saul was dead and that a new king was now ruling.

Regardless of the decisions made, the church would have to keeping moving in order to

be effective for the kingdom. The pastor elaborated on the following three points. They

are: 1. Keep being on one accord, 2. Maximize your every moment, 3. Preparation for a

progressive work. When the congregation embraced these three tenets, they then could

celebrate in the Lord Jesus Christ. The connection of this sermon to module one sanctions

a need for SJBC to follow leadership by walking together harmoniously for kingdom

progression. This module consists of five lessons.

In Module 2 Deacon Roles and Responsibilities, the pastor taught from a sermon

entitled, "What the Word Will Do", (APPENDIX N 2). In that sermon, the pastor

discusses not being in the will of God and the chaos and confusion that results. Just as

Ezekiel spoke of being the watchmen for the people, so are the deacons at SJBC to be so,

in collaboration with the pastor. This sermon connects with this module by having the congregants to position ourselves for God's next move. We must take an assessment of our lives, recognizing our responsibilities one to another. The module consists of five lessons.

Module 3 is Spiritual Disciplines. In this sermon, "Strength in the Journey", (APPENDIX N 3), the pastor questions why good things happen to bad people and conversely, why bad things happen to good people. As a spiritual discipline, deacons must have a productive prayer life, be able to witness and know that God is sovereign. Praise is a part of this process. Though our lives seem to be unproductive, we can still be joyful in God our Savior. The module consists of ten lessons.

Module 4 is Basic Ministry Skills. In the sermon, "The Perfect Posture for Ministry", (APPENDIX N 4), the pastor looks at how we conduct ministry. Our ministry seems basic when compared to ministries on the other side of town. Jesus can perfect even our most basic form of worship, of serving. Our training may not be the greatest, but it is what we can unashamedly offer God. We must have a hunger for the Word, realizing all of us have something of use for the kingdom, which allows God to transform our failures into opportunities. Church hurt was a constant theme in the ministry. Knowledge of how a church can unknowingly hurt its pastor and the vision is addressed. The researcher taught measures to protect church unity, while remaining a fruitful congregation. The module consists of 19 lessons.

Lastly, the pastor formulated the 5th module, "Deacon Partnership with the Pastor," as a means to preach, "What Real Friends Do", (APPENDIX N 5). In this sermon, the pastor espoused the importance of friendship. The pastor challenged leadership to be sensitive to each other, to make a decision in faith and to realize you are blessed to bless. That is the collaborative process required as the deacon and pastor co-labor in the vineyard together. This is the partnership, the connection necessary as the two journeys together reflecting one heart working for, with and in the kingdom. This module consists of six lessons .The complete training model has 46 lesson plans.

Through Ministry Development and interspersed throughout these trainings are a variety of communal trainings and activities where all of the membership can actively participate. This includes ministry fairs, guests and health response teams, community give-away, etc. SJBC's Hour of Power is one of the great culminations of these experiences. The pastor elaborated and taught on tithing every Sunday morning, encouraging all to "Try God. If it doesn't work, you can go back to doing what you were before." Ministry fairs were introduced to help new members, in particular, to discover where they could work in the ministry. The community give away was another means to evangelize. Members brought gently used clothing to share with the surrounding community, free of charge, as much as they would like to take. The Guest's Response team greets the guests that are worshipping with us and follows up in an effort to bring them into the fold. The Health Care and Response team was established to meet and respond to the health care needs of the congregation. The SJBC Hour of Power is the church's for intercessory prayer time held monthly on the fourth Saturday in the month.

Beyond the Title

The experiences of this teaching training moved the deacons beyond the title of 'deacon'. It moved it toward a collaborative partnership, meeting the needs of the people. The researcher was astutely aware of those areas that were detrimental to the harmony of kindred hearts. A careful approach to a solution had to be strategized. This strategy involved listening to the hurt and concerns of those congregants/deacons who had been inflicted with the harsh actions from other congregants, both intentional and unintentional. The researcher developed a posture of listening by not readily responding to anyone who may have been the victim or the perpetrator of some church offense or misconduct. Though the researcher was constantly approached daily with the congregants own perspective of what is right and what is wrong, their words could not penetrate the words of the Savior, Jesus when he said, "My sheep listen to my voice, and I know them and they follow me" (John 10:27). Following the voice of Jesus played a key role in not allowing the voices of the oppressed to dictate to the researcher the decision as to how to build relationships, or who and who not to build relationships with. In Romans, Paul saw servant leaders as co-laborers in Christ (Romans 16:3, 9). The researcher discerned the deacons in this same capacity, well enough to know their strengths and weaknesses. The researcher built relationships with the deacons as they began to further respect and trust the leadership. One strategy the researcher constantly employed was that of nurturing and sincerely commending publicly those who co-labored in the vineyard. Creditability with the deacons and congregation were critical byproducts of that partnership. These binding, connecting experiences subsequently led to the development of kindred spirits among the deacon/pastor ministry. These relationships were all based on equal footing, promoting the essence of a godly team. This was servant leadership at its best. In Chapter IV the researcher discussed what was done during the

development phase of the Deacon Training Model at SJBC. Chapter V will now focus on

the actual implementation process and its delivery.

CHAPTER V

FIELD EXPERIENCE

The field experience in Chapter V will detail the processes used to implement the Deacon Training Model. This model project has attempted to formulate an intensive plan of study for the deacon ministry, ascertaining what the researcher actually did in the project. During the implementation stage, the researcher had to establish a systematic means to train the then twenty-two deacons. Four deacons transitioned to be with the Lord during the pastor's tenure. The field experience consisted of approximately 46 sessions with the deacons. Even before these sessions were possible, much time was spent in healing church hurt within the congregation after a much divided church was at odds. The church, though attempting to remain together, was in upheaval. Prior to the trainings, the researcher met individually with the deacon members. Each had their own story to be told. Each deacon had experienced the turmoil in their own way. A sure and defined line of demarcation had been drawn. Church polity was under attack.

Beginnings of the Field Experience

The researcher knew that the first state of business had to be concerted prayer for the church family, particularly the deacon leadership. The deacons were weary in well-doing. Their experiences, some justified, some not, were very real. The researcher called the church to prayer from May 2011 through the entire 2012 calendar year. An Intercessory Prayer Team was then established as a continual monthly discipline for the entire congregation. It continues even today. The team consisted of ten leaders including associate ministers, deacons, deaconesses, trustees, and lay leaders. From the very start, the monthly one hour prayer session made an impact with each having 75-100 members in attendance. The need was great and sincere. Over the course of the first several months, the atmosphere in the church began to shift. A light feeling permeated the air as testified by several church members and from the leadership. The flock was beginning to experience a sense of peace. The tide was beginning to turn after the first year of the pastor's tenure.

Results of Intercessory Prayer Implementation

After the first full year of intercessory prayer that began in January 2012, every fourth Saturday, from 9:00 am to10:00 am, the church was now postured for the specialized training it so desperately needed. From the intercessory prayer time came a bible study on prayer with the deacons and laity. A formidable result of the intercessory prayer was better communication between and among the deacons. Also small group bible sessions in other ministries were initiated and continued. Moreover, prayer partners were established, enhanced and remained in covenant relationships. With progressive growth, membership is now able to send their prayer request to the prayer ministry electronically, a 21st century church characteristic. The intercessory prayer ministry continues to be a vital part of the overall SJBC ministry and culture.

Deacon Training

The researcher began with general planned trainings for the deacons. However, this became more specific when the interest level of the participants generated a need for more sessions. The more the deacons were taught, the more they realized the need for additional and continual training. The training began with leadership, specifically the deacon ministry first. Later, the laity was requesting similar training. Thus, the researcher developed planned trainings with dual audiences. There were several considerations in mind as he set the stage for the training. These considerations were the spiritual maturation level of the deacon and their specific knowledge regarding instruction. Emphasis was placed on the partnership required between the pastor and deacon board. Additionally, transforming the thought process of the deacon from one of resting on the church's previous laurels to meeting the diverse needs of the congregation was pivotal. This led to one of the modules entitled Deacon Partnership with the Pastor. Governance of the church became an air of contention particularly after previous leadership experiences. However, the receptivity to training from the Word of God eradicated that schism.

Ministry Development

Various ministries developed after training proceeded. These included the development of the Vision Team, Media Ministry, Clothing Give-Away and the Vacation Bible School (both held at a local housing development) to name a few. These new ministries helped to re-establish the church's good reputation in the community. SJBC, historically, was known for its service ministries within its high needs community. With the infusion of a dynamic pastor who was sensitive to the needs of the sheep, the church was ready to re-gain its footing as a source for true, God-breathed ministry. Inclusive in this project was the use of group interviews, observations, focus groups, surveys, and questionnaires.

Collection of Qualitative Data

After an examination of the scriptures and some initial leadership training of the deacons, the researcher prepared a time informally interviewing a variety of stakeholders attempting to ascertain perceptions of the needs of the church and the community. Additionally, there were informal interviews with church and community members about their concerns. Simultaneously interviews took place with other church leaders about their deacon models of training. The researcher also used pre and post assessments to survey the deacon's knowledge of their roles and responsibilities. As previously stated in chapter 4, the researcher gathered anecdotal notes from observations and discussions during deacon and church meetings where lack of communication among them and the congregation surfaced. Also notes from the interactions of the members with each other during church services and other social settings were also information that was collected.

Stakeholders Group Interview Questionnaire Results

1. What are the strengths of the church?

Stakeholders spoke of the past accomplishments of the church, specifically feeding and housing the homeless, subsidized housing, housing for the elderly, a daycare center, a nursing home and that the church was debt-free, just to name a few. Of the 30 stakeholders interviewed, all mentioned at least two of the above accomplishments. It was evident there was a sense of pride that radiated in the group because of these accomplishments.

2. What are some areas, you believe, the church could improve?

Of the 30 respondents, half felt the church needed improvement in communication. They spoke of factions existing within the church. Five cited specific incidents they had witnessed first-hand where communication failed or was misinterpreted. When challenged as to what they did to counter the problem they witnessed, it was even more evident their silence suggested they did not intervene during or even after the miscommunication.

3. What new ministries or teachings would you like to see?

There was not a consensus. However, a few mentioned the need for more involvement of young adults in church functions. The young adults ages 18-35 had left the church over the years especially during the time without a pastor. The musicians wanted better instruments. The choirs wanted better robes. The researcher observed that not one of the 30 participants mentioned evangelism as even a consideration. Problems were the focus and not the means to systematically address those specific problems. Also, one-third of the stakeholders expressed a desire to transform the Sunday devotional period with a more progressive and involved means of worship. As a result, a praise team was formed who currently ministers every Sunday morning before each service.

4. What is the vision/mission of the church?

None of the interviewees could articulate a mission statement. The church did not have one. The Vision Team would later develop Mission and Vision Statements. This process lasted over a period of eight months. The previous Pastoral Search Committee had been transformed into the Vision Team. The pastor met with the committee, consisting of three deacons and the remaining 12 were leaders in the overall SJBC ministry. The pastor used the book, *'Developing a Vision for Ministry in the 21ˢᵗ Century'* by Aubrey Malphurs, as the book study for the group. During and after the book study, the team began the process of developing out the church's current Mission and Vision Statements. It was later presented to the church body for further review. The congregation voted to accept the recommendations during a quarterly church conference. The Vision and Mission statements are listed as follows:

- SJBC's Mission Statement: A Discipling Church Ministering Through Reaching, Preaching and Teaching

- SJBC's Vision Statement: St. James Baptist Church seeks to reach the lost through preaching and teaching the inerrant word of God, equipping believers through discipleship and ministering to the body of Christ through the use of our spiritual gifts while serving Jesus Christ and the needs of others.

5. What leadership roles do women occupy in the ministry?

Twenty-five of the 30 participants identified women ushers, Sunday School Superintendent and teachers and the culinary committee as positions women held. The researcher noted none mentioned the deaconess because this position is not considered one of leadership. A deaconess is considered only as the wife of the deacon with no authority. This point will be addressed in Chapter VI.

6. What training opportunities have you been a part of in the last three years?

Eighty-five percent of the stakeholders stated they had not participated in any training within the last three years. The trainings were cut because of fewer resources and less income coming in and the church still did not have a pastor during those times. The participants desired a more planned program of study and training that directly met their individual and the church's collective needs.

7. What training opportunities would you like to see?

Seventy-five percent wanted trainings specific to their ministry or areas of leadership.

Deacons wanted training specifically from the pastor, not from outside consultants. For

whatever reason, 9 of the 15 deacons desired to be trained initially by their pastor.

Hearing from their Man of God was important. Since the pastor was new to the SJBC

family, the deacons present were adamant about their choices. They, however, were not

opposed to other outside consultants/preachers coming in to help train later, but they

wanted the pastor to first set the foundation. The pastor also noted that of the 15 deacons

present, 8 of them stated they felt they had been adequately trained over the years for

service. These deacons held their current positions for over 25 years.

As a result of the information gathered from the group interview, the pastor later

conferred with two other local pastors. These two pastors were instrumental in coming in

to check on the church while they were without a pastor. These pastors shared their

knowledge of the church over the years, its challenges over the last few years and its

potential for continued growth. Their assessment suggested this church was fertile

ground for seriously significant transformation. The church, from its history to the

present, would be able to rebound with a structured approach to training.

As a result of findings from the qualitative and quantitative sources, recurring

themes/patterns surfaced during this introspection. These themes/patterns were:

1. Some disagreement on the need for deacon training among some veteran
    deacons.

2. Complacency with the accomplishments of the past good deeds.

3. Church operations steeped in tradition. Deacons opened up service with devotion that seemed routine, mundane and less inviting.

4. Lack of a mission and vision statement for the church.

5. Lack of trust within the congregation of the deacons that surfaced during church conferences.

6. Varying levels of spiritual maturity and/or knowledge as evidenced by appropriate means to handle conflict.

With this information, the researcher also analyzed Paul's epistle to Timothy and Titus. Biblically, there are few specific references as to what a deacon does. SJBC's deacon ministry has been a product of a more generalized interpretation of their roles.

Churches Deacon Model Interviews

The researcher and contextual associates interviewed representatives from three of the five model churches. Some of the key questions posed were:

1. Describe the demographics of your congregation.

   Ebenezer Baptist Church (EBC): 53 deacons which includes twelve women, ranging from ages 32-92, approximately 5,000 plus members, many community professionals attend the church

   Shalom—6 deacons, 250 members, reflective of mixed ages, particularly young adults, multi-cultural

   Love and Faith—1,500 members with 20 deacons, professional cross section of people; strong young adult ministry

2. Do you have a diaconal ministry?

EBC—yes

Shalom—yes

Love and Faith—yes

3. What type trainings have you conducted for the diaconal ministry?

   EBC trainings are 1.5 hours, consisting of 12-15 sessions within the topic areas.

   Topic areas include Christian Doctrine, Governance, History, etc.

   Shalom trainings are taught in a series of one-word promises (example:

   Manifestations, Praise) with accommodating scriptures

   Love and Faith trainings---Evangelism, Fruit of the Spirit, Spiritual Gifts

4. Does your church have a formalized training program for the deacon/diaconal

   ministry?

   EBC—yes

   Shalom—yes

   Love and Faith---yes

5. Does your church have a Family Care Ministry?

   EBC—yes, by zip codes

   Shalom—yes, by zones

   Love and Faith—yes, by zones

6. Do your deacons rotate? If so, what is the rotation?

   EBC—do not rotate, but do have some on emeritus status

   Shalom—no

   Love and Faith—no

7. Is your training pastor-led?

EBC—yes, but some are conducted by the Deacon Board chairman

Shalom—yes

Love and Faith—yes

Pre- and Post-Assessments

The researcher used a pre- and post-assessment as a means to measure the deacon's perceptions and understanding of their roles and responsibilities. The questions were:

1. What do you consider to be the role and responsibilities of the deacon?

   Initially, half of the eighteen deacons believed their primary role was to give communion, count money and visit the sick. After the involvement of training on the Pastor and Deacon Relationship and the Roles and Responsibilities of the Deacons, ninety-five percent understood the deacons had a vital part as co-laborers in the ministry. This is an example cited as how they could do their work better. As in Exodus 17, the deacons were to lift the pastor's arms while he served.

2. On a scale of 1-10, with 1 being the least and 10 being the highest, how effective are you in each of the following areas after deacon training?

	Pre-Assessment	Post-Assessment
Problem-Solving	8	8
Prayer Life	7	9
Teaching	4	6
Love and Commitment	10	10

| Confidentiality | 6 | 9 |
| Conflict Resolution | 7 | 9 |

3. What are you currently doing to meet the spiritual needs of the community?

   Thirteen of the deacons initially mentioned the church's Vacation Bible School, Sunday School and regular church service. After training, 16 of the 18 deacons mentioned evangelism, prayer vigils and the community Vacation Bible School.

4. What do you believe to be the role of the pastor?

   Before training, the pastor's role was thought to be that of preaching, teaching Bible Study and visiting the sick. After training, 100% of the deacons believed the pastor's role to be one of a partnership in meeting the needs of the church congregation. They understood the importance of serving together to address the needs of the congregation.

5. How would you describe the 21st century church? Ninety-seven percent initially described the 21st century church as needing more technology. After training, the focus was more ministering to the multi-generations and non-traditional families of the church. The researcher knew, according to this data, he had to extend his teachings to cover such topics.

6. What leadership roles do you see women performing in the church?

   The pre- and post-assessments did not change regarding women in diaconal leadership. All of the deacons cited women ministers/preachers as a leadership role. Therefore, the researcher had to delay training plans in order to eventually include women as an equal part of the deacon ministry. Until then, more training would be needed. A deaconess was not considered as part of church leadership; they were simply the wives of the deacons.

In 'To Deacon or Not to Deacon,' the 26 stakeholders, (associate ministers, office/ staff, deacon and deaconesses), all cited the following as primary roles and responsibilities of the deacons at SJBC. The top ten are as follows:

1. Daily prayer and devotion time

2. Regular and consistent attendance in Sunday School and/or Bible Study

3. Regular and consistent giving of tithes and offerings

4. Developing a spiritual growth program for the congregation

5. Supporting the pastor and the vision God has given him

6. Assisting in conducting the ordinances of the church

7. Taking communion to/visiting the healing and recovering

8. Continual spiritual training as a unified deacon ministry

9. Recognizing and using your spiritual gifts

10. Conducting a Deacon Family Care Ministry

Deacon Trainings Implemented

Formal and informal deacon trainings occurred monthly. Interspersed throughout the church calendar were quarterly church-wide leadership conferences. The trainings lasted from two to five hours, depending on the subject matter and audience. The researcher used the Word of God to convict hearts and minds regarding praise and worship, tithes and offerings, prayer and fasting, Bible Study and Sunday School and loving each other God's way. Sunday School had historically served as the premier

Christian Education authority in the church. Each of the 15 Sunday school classes has four teachers. Members of the deacon ministry, approximately 83%, were regular and consistent Sunday School attendees (APPENDIX E). This tended to be where much of the core of the church received instruction. Morning worship services were next in line for the highest level of attendance for trainings or teachings.

Last, the qualitative data emanating from the surveys suggested the deacon leaders came into the ministry many times because they were asked. Approximately 40% of the deacons, who served in the office for 25 years or more, especially if SJBC had been their church home since childhood, were most likely hand-selected because they were deemed good guys and their families knew each other. Veteran deacons were seen as the epitome of 'what a good deacon should be.' Five of the 18 deacons are new to the ministry. The pastor spent one full year training and further introducing the novices to the deaconship. These new deacons, coincidentally, had an advantage of initial training that the veteran deacons did not. Once realizing the needs based on feedback, this opportunity was extended to the full deacon ministry. Additionally, those new deacons over the year of training, got to experience firsthand the pastor's expectations through scripture, coupled with understanding his heart for this great work in ministry. This training, however, was not as extensive as this proposed model suggests. Yet, the formal introduction of this training was critical to helping the deacon ministry to get off to the right start.

The researcher developed and began the initial stages of instituting a three-year plan of study for the deacon ministry. The first year focused primarily on prayer. Before that first year ended, small, but organized studies began. Having an intimate time to garner the strength and talents of leadership was necessary to having the church move forward. Some of the sessions could be completed in just one workshop time period, while others may have to be spread over several sessions. The researcher allowed group dynamics to determine how slow or fast they would proceed. The concern was not so much how quickly they moved from module to module, but rather the spiritual nuggets that were being gleaned as a result. Teachable moments were celebrated and embraced.

In order to transform the deacons, the sessions became mini-Bible Studies through default. The researcher knew he had to further undergird them in scripture in order for them to become stronger servant leaders. The requirements needed for the deacons were no longer their father's church from days of old. It was now a progressive ministry model that went far beyond what they originally were taught. The church was now positioned to be transformed inside out and in its people. Acts 6 was beginning to become alive and well within the hearts and minds of the deacons. The researcher believed when the deacon became empowered biblically, they would become a force to be reckoned with in and outside the church community. This seemed to be the starting point for a similar heart ready for productive service. Their hearts and the pastor's heart were now knitted through the Word of God, with a common purpose. This deacon/pastor partnership set the stage for transformation of the deacon ministry. The pastor involved the Contextual Associates to assist in preparing and extending this relationship with resources.

Introduction of the Contextual Associates

The Contextual Associates were critical in the development and coordination of training seminars. They helped the researcher locate, pull resources and assured that the ministry goals all aligned with the vision statement. In so doing, they helped the researcher stay focused on the planned objectives for training. Their level of involvement was clearly defined after the researcher met with them to outline the goals and vision for the Doctor of Ministry Project entitled, "A Partnership of Similar Hearts: A Collaborative Approach to Deacon/Pastor Ministry at St. James Baptist Church". They assisted with resource identification and selection based on the particular module being addressed and taught. Therefore, 46 individual deacon groups and church-wide sessions were conducted.

Contextual Associates helped the pastor disaggregate the evaluation data from the church-wide conferences and assisted in analyzing results from the "To Deacon or Not To Deacon" survey (APPENDIX J). Primarily, the Contextual Associates served as the unofficial thought processors and provokers for the researcher as the research progressed. They challenged the researcher's thinking regarding the proposed training module. The researcher had to clearly articulate the vision for the project with precision and authority.

Being cognizant of the various skillsets represented within the deacon ministry, the researcher shared information with the Contextual Associates for the sole purpose of planning for training and being readily cognizant of the deacon ministry. Together, they formulated a plan of action to address those areas while simultaneously building capacity in and through others.

Lesson Design Description

Lesson design was a critical piece of the training model. For the deacons, there was a range of educational levels from those formally degreed to those who were high school graduates. Others presented a more reserved demeanor while operating and serving under the radar in the ministry itself. These men were not as vocal when having to take a position for or against a decision. With that in mind, the researcher planned sessions that would meet all levels of learning.

The diverse educational levels within the church were a different challenge. The church was home to persons who were functionally illiterate or could barely read fluently, to those with advanced professional degrees. The researcher had to adjust the presentation style and design by coupling both open discussion with actually reading text to the group. Interestingly enough, regardless of the audience, the researcher's style (infused with humor), broke down barriers to learning. The church members were able to relax and receive the unadulterated Word of God. The researcher had met the congregation where they were, and in so doing, provided an avenue to propel them higher in the knowledge and saving grace of our Lord and Savior, Jesus Christ.

After the trainings, the researcher reviewed the evaluations and fine-tuned future preparations with those recommendations (APPENDIX O). The evaluation instrument would prove to serve as a critical piece of data. This allowed the presentations to remain cutting edge as the leadership was taught. Exercises whereby the deacons prioritized their roles and responsibilities, was an eye-opener for the researcher. Eighteen deacons had a wide array of opinions as to what was most important in their servant ministry. Their interpretations were all over the place. When the deaconess, staff/others and ministers were given the same instrument, they too had a wide spread of opinions as to what roles were most important in the deacon ministry. The researcher took the results and attempted to triangulate the resulting data. The researcher identified ten duty areas where all of the groups did agree (APPENDIX P**). That information was used to customize future training opportunities for the deacons. It was imperative that all the stakeholders and laity understand the essential roles needed for the deacons to become effective leaders. This process was collaborative in nature and could assist future deacons in determining their readiness for service.

Deacon Focus Groups

One of the greatest highlights garnered from this training experience was the deacon focus group. Approximately ten members of the deacon ministry met 90 minutes prior to a church-wide training to answer questions regarding their deacon experiences (APPENDIX K). Each group member recollected how they became a deacon and how they learned to be a deacon. Several recounted they became deacons because they were asked. Very few mentioned the Acts 6 or 1 Timothy 3 scriptures as their initial foundation. Several were told to "follow and do what the other more veteran deacons did." This was their 'on the job training.' The researcher now had a better understanding why the Lord was leading him to conduct these training sessions and why the model had to be set up as the Lord designed. There was a tremendous need because lives were at stake. Deacon ministry was no longer considered an office but rather a ministry for the people. It was servant leadership at its best. The Word was now the change agent. Hearts were not just knitted together; they were now collaborating for a common vision in ministering to God's people at SJBC.

The Deacon Profile Interview questions were as follows:

1. How did you come to SJBC?

2. How long have you been a deacon?

3. What is your definition of a deacon?

4. What do you believe are your spiritual gifts?

5. What or how would you describe the mission of the church?

6. What would you like to see changed in the deacon ministry?

Lessons Along the Way

There were a few surprises along the way. The researcher knew even before accepting this assignment, that the sheep had been critically injured, particularly the deacons. That humbling encounter left the researcher in constant prayer. The Holy Spirit steered the SJBC ship of Zion to safe, less tumultuous waters. There were days God told the researcher to go forward in battle. There were other days the researcher was told to take a 'not right now' stance. This obedient countenance required the Lord to provide for the needs of the church. God shored up the leaning post so that the researcher could secure solid footing, while conducting training for the deacons. The researcher, however, was consistent in doing what God told him to do with respect to training. The directive was still the same for the researcher. That directive was "you move when I move. We will follow God's lead." This also allowed the researcher to bring in those scattered sheep who had previously left the church. Through the collaborative efforts of the deacon and pastor, they collectively sought out and encouraged those persons to return home to SJBC. This is a true example of co-laboring for Christ in the ministry.

The researcher began to organize the scattered sheep for ministry. We all, like sheep, have gone astray. Each of us has turned to our own way; and the Lord has laid on him the iniquity of us all (Isaiah 53:6). This created an atmosphere now to receive a common vision for ministry. The congregants were hungry yearning for manna. The researcher understood that hunger, and through Christ, began to continually feed them the Word of God. This manna was able to nurture and prepare them for the unity of transition needed.

CHAPTER VI

SUMMARY, CONCLUSIONS, RECOMMENDATIONS

Chapter VI focuses on the summary learning, reflections encountered and conclusions drawn while conducting and completing this project. This has been one remarkable journey. The researcher never imagined the complexity of researching this idea of deacon training while attempting to customize it to meet the needs of St. James Baptist Church, and establish a partnership between deacons and pastor. The conditions that were present in the church community were strongholds that required immediate and appropriate attention. It became obvious that no form of training would be received until the researcher was able to help begin restoring strained relationships. Trust and faith were on the line. The researcher used the Word of God as the balm for healing the pervasive hurt encircling the camp. When the Holy Spirit made the conditions right, the researcher began to carefully and strategically introduce the need for training.

There was no resistance when the idea of training was introduced. However, the overall objective as to who the training was intended was unclear. The researcher asked that the leadership be present for the training. It became evident that the use of the term 'leadership' in the SJBC context had multiple meanings. For instance, some thought leadership was just the current deacon board. Others thought it referred to the presidents of the different ministries. Others thought it was the chairman of the deacon board and the chairman of the finance committee. The church now had incumbent deacons and deacons-in-training. A point of clarification had to be made. It had been more than ten years since the church previously ordained any deacons. A more inclusive group was now defined as the leadership who required training. The 'leadership' referenced in this project included the deacons ministry and to some extent, ministry presidents. However, ministry presidents did not make governing decisions or allocate finances.

When the training program first began, the excitement was incredulous and lasted throughout all the pastor-led instruction. The leadership was awed by having a structured program and that the training would be pastor-led. Having 'their' pastor conduct the training was joy beyond measure. The leaders now had a vested interest in their own spiritual growth and development. Regardless, the training still needed to have an evaluation instrument to measure the trainings' effectiveness. There was not an evaluation initially, yet subsequent trainings would be evaluated.

The number of deacons in the actual trainings increased as instruction continued as evidenced by the sign-in sheets. The training was shared via print and electronic media. If trainings were missed, the deacons still were accountable for the information shared. The pastor would follow up with those absent to ensure they received the necessary information. The ability to replicate this project in a variety of settings is strong and formed a partnership of similar hearts between the deacon and pastor at SJBC.

Summary

This project has attempted to better refine a more uniform way to train the deacons in ministry. It helped the deacons to administer their charge most effectively while sharing similar hearts with the pastor. SJBC has had a history of continued education throughout the years. However, that training historically has been basic and sporadic not yielding the needed changes. Emphasis for the deacon has been more related to 'maintaining the facility' rather than developing the spiritual growth of the congregants.

With varying levels of deacon astuteness, the church has successfully maintained the status quo (doing things the way we have always done it) with no problem. Transforming the ministry into a more involved, spiritual entity has been the desired effect for kingdom building. The researcher believes it is essential that the deacon ministry fully embraces its scriptural charge, not just as an office, but truly as servants. In order to effectively minister to the needs of the diverse families at SJBC, it is critically important that the deacons know, understand and can apply scripture to the gaping, bleeding wounds of the sheep.

SJBC is a strong, loving church that initially, was not fully aware of the deacons' need to receive intense training. They functioned well administratively: taking care of its finances, maintaining its ministries and securing the needs of the physical building. Yet, the same fervor was not present when it came to building a foundational training base and more for its leadership. The church, primarily consisting of members ages fifty plus, seemed content in business as usual. 'The men' were handling the business of church. However, the purpose of the deacon ministry as evidenced in Acts 6 seemed to fade. For a period of several years when the church was without a pastor, attempts to take care of the infirmed and the widows meagerly existed. The deacons were trying to stay afloat and have the church stay together. New members began to leave and veteran members' confidence in the leadership began to erode. The church was at a crossroad and training was nowhere near the top of the list of priorities. A 'learn-as-I-go' mindset was prevalent. This training model has attempted to transform that mindset to one of servanthood. Subsequently, several transformations have already been interjected in the ministry including the following transitions:

Deacon-led Devotion and Testimony Service to Praise and Worship Team: The church had an extensive history of the deacons conducting the Sunday morning devotional at each service. The standard was to read the scripture, pray and perhaps sing a song. As the church body grew, they wanted to become more a part of the service, with a mix of contemporary and hymnal praise and worship music. Devotion began to take on a more energetic and involved praise and worship time. The congregation was far more engaged and participated.

Auxiliaries and Committees to Ministries: The character of the auxiliaries and committees seemed too business formal, with little expression of spirituality while making decisions. The transformation came as a result of teachings on the vision and mission statements which emphasized correlating every aspect of service to ministry. No longer was this just a name of a group of people meeting. It now was a group of people in service for our Lord and Savior.

A Select few making decisions to Stakeholders Involvement: Oftentimes, it seemed as though the deacons and finance committee were making all the decisions. While they were charged to do so, they began to seek the opinion of the body more frequently, especially in matters that would have had far more reaching ramifications on the total church.

Exclusive Use of KJV to Use of NKJV, NIV, The Message Bible: The church, for over many years, only used the King James Version of the bible. There appeared to be an unspoken notion of many in the church body that you must be able to understand the King James Version in order to 'rightly divide.' With the onslaught of many previously un-churched persons now joining the church, the pastor began to use a variety of bible styles that would better connect with the congregation. The pastor would read the King James Version and perhaps, the New International version. The goal was that the scripture became alive and well for all who read and heard.

Female-dominated ushers to now include an All-Male Ushers Ministry: SJBC always had a strong male presence. However, they were not as involved in the ministry. The pastor created an all-male usher board, The King's Men, who have transformed that mindset and has been the catalyst for other men becoming more involved in other ministries.

No symbol to define the church to a member designed church logo: SJBC had no logo. There was nothing to identify the church visually, other than being the church on the corner of Randleman and West Florida Street. The Vision committee, working in concert with the pastor and other members, researched, created and designed the symbol that represents the church.

Sick and Shut-In to Healing and Recovery: Perhaps semantics to some, the transformation in title from sick and shut-in to healing and recovery, was another transformation of faith. Sick and shut-in sounded so final. However, healing and recovery suggested more progress and a quest toward a more positive life, regardless of the ailment or infirmity.

Monthly 'Deacons Only' Prayer Time to Congregational Intercessory Prayer: While in the difficult days of the church without a pastor, a few deacons began meeting every Saturday morning at 6:00 to pray. As they became more encouraged, a natural progression of faith, emanated throughout the church community. Others wanted to participate, to be a part. The pastor, through prayer, introduced Intercessory Prayer for all once monthly. This Hour of Power, as it is called, has been one of the best transformations that the church has experienced.

The work involved in this project was multifaceted. Not only did the researcher have to unify a divisive church community, but also instill a sense of leadership that was representative for all the congregants. The researcher had to be slow, methodical and strategic while attempting to remain objective. Tremendous work revolved around addressing the needs of the deacons, re-establishing the position of spiritual leader and providing structure on a tumultuous ground. With all that, SJBC was at a stagnant place in the ministry, requiring sincere prayer.

Retrospectively, the researcher spent his first year observing and getting to know the church and the greater Greensboro community. That year of observation was well needed underscoring that training was essential. That training had to evolve from very basic concepts to more substantive education. Training was not only educational, but also had to be, relational. The researcher had to establish and maintain an intimate relationship with all, being open, yet making decisions based on the Word of God. There was no way the ministry would have been able to show its growth potential until there was a meeting of the minds. The researcher had to be the primary conduit for bridging that immense gap. A one on one meeting with the chairperson of the Deacons Ministry was the initial starting point. Then there were meetings with the deacons, followed by the greater church body. The meetings yielded evidence and an opportunity for identifying needed trainings. Therein, the training model for this project was birthed.

The researcher was well aware of the need to be systematic in the Christian Education delivery. Initially, the researcher planned for 10 extensive areas of training, or modules, to be conducted over a five year period. Im his first full year of his pastorate, it became abundantly clear that that goal was extremely ambitious. To remedy this, the researcher combined some of the trainings into a more cursory and succinct package. More importantly, the leadership was still healing and was not ready for too heavy a transformation, at least, not yet. The researcher came back to the drawing board with the deacons, reviewed and adjusted the progress and made plans to proceed with the then more current information.

As to the evaluating of the work, the researcher believed it was imperative that he took the allotted time to transition the deacon to a mindset for training. Church hurt and distrust was too prevalent for any understanding of the Word to become purposeful. So, though the need for the teaching of the Word was primary, the physical, spiritual and emotional well-being of the flock was paramount for unity. For which of you, if your son ask for bread, will give him a stone? (Matthew 7:9). The issue of women in leadership, particularly serving as deacons, is a thought that had not been fully explored at SJBC. The church body is comfortable with women serving in current capacities. There are female associate ministers, missionaries and Sunday School teachers, to name a few. Thorough training over a period of time will be necessary in order that women serving as deacons with all the inherent rights and responsibilities will be fully embraced. However, efforts to march toward that goal are still operational and in full effect.

The researcher, however, would do a few things differently. First and far most, he would call leadership to organized prayer bimonthly or weekly. He believed the healing had to occur from the top down before it could permeate throughout the church body. Organized prayer would have caused hearts to soften and minds to be able to hear the voice of God. That constant circle of prayer could then transfer down and throughout other church leaders. With that transfer of such holy power, it would not be long before everyone who sat in the pews or even entered through the threshold, would be better able to relax their hearts and allow the Holy Spirit to do His surgery.

Second, the researcher would attend as many ministry meetings as possible to continue setting the tone for open dialogue and communication. The church has over 30 active ministries. Though this task seems impossible, even impractical, it would be germane to fostering the biblical direction for the church family. When the body sees the pastor purposefully attempting to be the bridge builder, when they see him extending the olive branch, when they see him providing and delivering training for the deacons and the church, it is far more likely that cliques and schisms will begin to erode and fade as memory never no more.

Last but not least is the notion of fully embracing what is needed and expected for 21st century ministry leadership. A 21st century church cannot occur if it is without the inclusion of women serving particularly as deacons. A true diaconate must be established at SJBC. Women have always been a vital part of the church community holding various positions; yet not deemed as leaders with all the rights and responsibilities inherent. It is both other women and traditional deacons who attempt to preserve the traditional face of the deacon ministry. With women being the majority in the Black Baptist church, in particular, it behooves the church family to resist this complacency of acceptance or silence. That silence stifles growth. It is critically important that women be readily accepted into the "boardroom" that have historically been led by men and remains male-dominated. SJBC has never even entertained the notion of women serving as part of a diaconate. Years ago, women were subordinate in just about every culture. Those roles were based on ignorance and power. The researcher fully believes the church is well on its way toward meeting that goal. It will be through the nudging of the Holy Spirit, training of the deacons and melting of the hearts that the church will see the greater good and fully commit to such an honor and responsibility.

The limitations of this study can be a challenge. Perhaps, those who choose to attempt replication can do so without as many challenges as the researcher faced. Presenting and conducting this model in the context of a congregation seeking to fulfill the will of God will be a blessing. On the other hand, an involved ministry facing such disrepair as SJBC would have to go through the same, if not similar, conditions in order to come out intact on the other side. These conditions were indicative of the stages of death, from shock and disability to eventual acceptance. The omission of any one step would be detrimental to the healing that needed to take root.

Reflections

1. The researcher realized one can only go as fast as the people can receive and absorb and apply the training. Understand this intensive training can be overwhelming (even though the need is great). It may be appropriate to initially have fewer modules and lessons. One can add more as the feedback from the evaluations suggests. Also, one may find it necessary to break up the modules within the model, moving from one module to the next intermittently. Just ensure that movement is aligned with your overall goals and the mission and vision of the church.

2. Prioritize what you will do in those areas of instruction that are critical to moving the ministry. As previously stated, use your data to determine the key areas of

training that must be done and done with fidelity. Adhere to your established timelines for the training as much as possible.

3. Remember, Rome was not built in a day. You may have to spend more time on a session than what was previously designed which is alright. Flexibility is essential in conducting this type training. Be open to feedback from the congregation as you start and stop.

4. You will find that as the excitement intensifies for training this will build momentum. The pastor should proceed with caution so that being overly ambitious does not derail the training model. The goal is to thoroughly teach, not just make the congregation have a warm feeling.

These seemed to be the most important reflections the researcher learned from the project's inception to its implementation. Another pastor and church may have different reflections; however, any and all reflections will become the next bit of information that will help direct the church in its next steps.

It is important that leaders know the Word of God better than they know the church's bylaws. However, knowledge above the bylaws should be understood as you make bold moves for kingdom building. Allow the bylaws to run the day in and day out operations of the church. Yield to the Word of God as the authority for kingdom living. If the two shall conflict, the Word of God is automatically the permanent default. When replicating this project, a pastor and church should consider the following:

1. **Assess the deacons' readiness**. Each deacon board, just as in other groups, has belief systems that sometimes can get in the way of in-depth training. Through

frank discussions, the pastor can use spiritual gift inventories and/or personality inventories to maximize strengths within the deacon ministry. With this information, the pastor can use a variety of teaching techniques and strategies that, perhaps, will serve as a beginning marker for training. Additionally, the pastor must be aware of the level of spiritual maturity that exists in each deacon individually and then collectively as a ministry unit. Use the above recommendations and informal interviews and interactions to ascertain who is ready for more leadership opportunities. This will be invaluable time and effort well-spent.

2. **Address any turmoil that exists.** This could and will have an adverse effect on the training process. Address it immediately and thoroughly. Involve key stakeholders. Pretending or ignoring such conflict will undermine your efforts to strengthen your leadership and training efforts.

3. **As pastor, spend more time listening.** Listening without judgment is just as important as knowing when to speak. The researcher spent the first year observing. One may think this is wasted time. The contrary is true. One is taught far more as the pastor listens without presupposition. Inference skills are a must when attempting to 'hear the hearts' of those one must lead.

4. **Effective communication is a two way proposition**. Choose to understand before you ask to be understood. Communication before, during and after training is paramount to maintaining a positive posture. One must never guess what the next step is. Have those whose hearts are knitted with yours to help keep the lines of communication open.

5. **Know the culture of the church community.** The tremendous opportunity to know and grow your church only will come when one takes the time to understand the culture in which they may be or operate. The church demographically may be as diverse as the next. Within each church, within each community, there are spoken and unspoken rules. The pastor must take time to understand those nuances and formulate a means to address those challenges within the church context, especially while training.

6. **Provide a planned framework for conducting training.** One must be open to making adjustments as needed. This model has built-in flexibility in it. This will allow the pastor to meet the needs of the deacon ministry as deemed appropriate and necessary. SJBC spent considerable time dealing with church hurt. These sessions sometimes went beyond the specified time period. This proved to be therapeutic in nature for some members. The goal was not to finish every aspect of the model as pre-planned. Rather, depending on the needs of the church at that specified time, the pastor could go more in-depth as deemed necessary. The framework was the same. The movement within the framework was not necessarily so.

7. **Allow the lessons within the modules to be the tool used to begin restoring faith, confidence and trust in one another.** The researcher used the 'turn and talk' method to begin creating dialogue between members (APPENDIX M). This simple method of interacting, allows members who knew very little about each other, to begin establishing relationships with each other. This is also a simple,

non-threatening method used for others to share what they think and feel about spiritual matters.

8. **Be ready to articulate your goals and objectives for the trainings**. Make sure they are S.M.A.R.T: specific, measurable, attainable, realistic and time sensitive.

9. **Evaluate, evaluate, evaluate**. Let your data speak for itself upon which you base your goals and objectives. Evaluations, whether formal or not, should be interspersed throughout the Deacon Training Model experience.

Conclusion

Finally, one must remember to meet the needs of the people right where they are. Training and development is only as good as the heart willing to receive it. Much effort can go into transforming the deacon, but it is imperative the pastor utilizes his advanced skill sets to harness every facet of the ministry. Letting one part die or barely thrive is a condition that cannot be tolerated. Additionally, training must be needs based and methodical because souls are at stake. Jesus told Simon Peter to cast his net on a certain side of the boat in order to gather the fish. Jesus recognized Simon Peter's intellect in fishing, but he did not need him to use what he knew. He needed Simon Peter and the other disciples to use what Jesus wanted him to use and just like He wanted him to use it. For SJBC, what they currently knew was confusion and distrust. The researcher had to address that state of being before any teaching, relevant to the deacon ministry, could be developed and further enhanced. SJBC now has "A Partnership of Similar Hearts: A Collaborative Approach to Deacon/Pastor Ministry".

BIBLIOGRAPHY

Anderson, Leith. "What Will the 21st Century Church Be Like?". *Enrichment Journal*. Accessed March 18, 2015 http://enrichmentjournal.ag.org/200001/026_21stcentury.cfm

Barton, Kyle. "Paradigm Change in Theology." *Conversant Faith,* September 18, 2012. Accessed October 16, 2014 http://conversantfaith.com/2012/09/18/paradigm-change-in-theology/html.

Boice, James. *An Expositional Commentary -ACTS*. Grand Rapids, MI: Baker Books, 1997.

Borg, Marcus J., and John Dominic Crossan. *The First Paul: Reclaiming the Radical Visionary Behind the Church's Conservative Icon*. New York, NY: HarperOne, 2010.

Breidenbough, Joel R. "Give Me a D-E-A-C-O-N! What's That Spell?" *First Baptist Sweetwater*. Accessed December 14, 2014. http://www.fbsweetwater.org/pdf/JoelsPublications.

Brochure on Collaborative Leadership. *United Theological Seminary 2003*. Accessed February 13, 2015 http://united.edu/collaborativeleadership.

Bruce, A.B. *The Training of the Twelve*. Cedar Lake, MI: Read a Classic Publishers, 2010.

Elliott Bryant. *Interview by Veronica Bryant*, Greensboro, NC, December 23, 2014.

Cambridge Greek New Testament for School and Colleges. *Study Light*. Accessed January 8, 2015 http://www.studylight.org.commentarys/cgt/view.cgl.

Christian Bible Reference Site, "What does the Bible Say about Women in Ministry" *Christian Bible Reference*. Accessed March 18, 2015 http://www.christianbiblereference.org/faq_women.htm.

City of Greensboro. *Living.* Accessed December 29, 2014 www.greensboro-nc.gov/.

Cole, Eric. *Interview by Veronica Bryant*. Greensboro, NC February 18, 2015.

Cottrell, David, and Lee J. Colan. *The Nature of Excellence*. Dallas, TX: CornerStone Leadership Institute, 2009.

Cowan, Kathy Moore. "The Graying of America: Preparing for What Comes Next." *Federal Reserve Bank of St. Louis*. Accessed March 18, 2015. https://www.stlouisfed.org/publications/bridges/fall-2013.

Cowen, Gerald. "The Role of the Dean." *Crosswalk.com*. Accessed October 10, 2014. http:/www.crosswalk.com/church/pastors-or-leadership/the-role-of-the-deacon-1235697.htm.

Daft, Richard, and Robert H. Lengel. *Fusion Leadership: Unlocking the Subtle Forces That Change People and Organizations.* San Francisco, CA: Berrett-Koehler, 2000.

Dashiff, Carol, Wendy DiMicco, Beverly Myers, and Kathy Sheppard. "Poverty and Adolescent Mental Health." *Journal of Child and Adolescent Psychiatric Nursing* 22, no. 25 (2009). Accessed March 9, 2015. http://www.onlinelibrary.wiley.com.

Ditewig, William T. *The Emerging Deacon*. New York, NY: Paulist Press, 1993.

Dodson, Jonathan. "Deacon Training-II (Practice of Deacons)." *Christ Is All-BLOG*. Accessed September 16, 2014. http://www.jonathandodson.org/2008/11/deacon-training-II.

Ellor, James W., and Michael E. Sherr. "Elder Mistreatment and the Church: Potential Roles for Helping Professionals and Congregations." *Social Work and Christianity* 36 (2009): 23. Accessed March 15, 2015. http://www.nascw.org.

Firmin, Michael W., and Jonathan W. Young. "Qualitative Perspectives toward Relational Connection in Pastoral Ministry." *The Qualitative Report* 19, no. 47 (2014): 1. Accessed March 15, 2015. http://www.nova.edu.sss/QR/QR19/young93.pdf.

Ford, Kevin, and Ken Tucker. *The Leadership Triangle*. New York, NY: James Publishing, 2013.

Foshee, Howard B. *Now That You're a Deacon*. Nashville, TN: B & H Books, 1975.

Geiger, Eric. *Transformational Discipleship: How People Really Grow*. Nashville, TN: B. & H. Books, 2012.

Gentle, Derek. "The Biblical Role of Deacons." *The Baptist Start Page:* 1-10. Accessed November 1, 2014. http://www.baptiststart.com/print/role_of_deacons.html.

Global Christian Center, "Challenges for the Twenty-First Church," Accessed March 18, 2015 https://globalchristiancenter.com/administrative-leadership/church-leadership/church-leadership/25079-challenges-for-the-21st-century-church.

Gool, Robyn. *Proper Attitudes Toward Leadership*. Tulsa, OK: Christian Publishing Services, 1987.

Grady, Carey A. "The Black Church." *African American Registry.* Accessed March 27, 2014. http:/www.aaregistry.org/historic-events/view/black-church-brief-history-html.

Guzik, David. "Commentary on Numbers 15:1". Accessed November 13, 2014 http://www.studylight.org/commentaries/guz/view.cgl?book=nu&chapter=015. 1997-2003.

Hammett, Edward H., and James R. Pierce. *Reaching People Under 40 While Keeping People Over 60.* Atlanta, GA: Chalice Press, 2007.

Harney, Kevin. *Leadership From the Inside Out.* Grand Rapids, MI: Zondervan, 2007.

Harris, James H. *The Word Made Plain* (Minneapolis: Augsburg Fortress, 2004), 39.

Helping Professionals and Congregations." *Social Work and Christians* 36 (2009).

Henderson, Trennis. Editor of Western Recorder, *News Journal of the Kentucky Baptist Convention.* Accessed April 7, 2015.

Heuser, Roger and Norman Shawchuck. *Leading the Congregation: Caring for Yourself While Serving Others* (Nashville, TN: Abington Press 1993), Kindle eBook.

Hill, E. V. *Victory in Jesus: Running the Race You Are Meant to Win.* Chicago, IL: Moody Publishers, 2003.

Hollinger, Tom. "Leadership Development and Succession Planning: A Biblical Perspective for an Ethical Response." *Journal of Biblical Prospective in Leadership* 5 (2013): 157-164.

Hurd, Seth Tower. "The Unexpected Things Millennials Want in Church." *Relevant Magazine* (November 2014). Accessed March 18, 2015. http://www.relevantmagazine.com.

Jackson, Rogers. *The Why of the Deacon.* Bel Air, CA: Cronos Press, 2012.

Jeremiah, David. *The Jeremiah Study Bible.* Brentwood, TN: Worthy Publishing, 2013.

_____. *The Formation of the Church, Volume 2.* San Diego, CA: Birmingham Press, 2007.

Johnson Sr., Lamont. *Autonomous: 21st Century Look at the African-American Baptist Church.* Newark, NJ: Godzchild Publication, 2011.

Keating, James. *The Deacon Reader.* New York, NY: Paulist Press, 2005.

Kroll, Paul. "Exploring the Book of Acts ." *Grace Communion International.* Accessed March 27, 2014. https://www.gci.org/bible/acts6.

Liautaud, Marian V. "5 Things Millenials Wish the Church Would Be," *Exponential.* Accessed March 18, 2015, http://www.exponential.org.

Lea, Thomas D. and Hayne P. Griffin, Jr. *The New American Commentary.* 1, 2 Timothy, Titus   Volume 34. Accessed November 14, 2014 www.olivetree.com/store/product.php?productid=17914.

Lemke, Steve. "How Deacons Can Help Their Pastors." *Baptist Message* 24, no. 12 (2009): 14.

Luper, Archie. "The Jethro Principle." *FaithSite.com.* Accessed March 14, 2015 http://cbti.faithsite.com

MacArthur, John. *Twelve Ordinary Men.* Nashville, TN: Thomas Nelson Publishers, 2003.

Mack, Natasha, Cynthia Woodsong, Kathleen MacQueen, Greg Guest, Emily Namey, *Qualitative Research Methods: A Data Collector's Field Guide* (Research Triangle Park, NC: Family Health International) 2005.

Maggio, Jennifer. Five Reasons Churches should serve Single moms. *Pastors.com.* May 17, 2012. Accessed March 14, 2015. www.pastors.com/5-reasons-your-church-should-serve- single-moms

Mallory, Sue, and Brad Smith. *The Equipping Church.* Grand Rapids, MI: Zondervan Publishers,   2001.

Malphurs, Aubrey. "Growing Leaders for Ministry in the 21st Century," *Enrichment Journal.* Accessed March 12, 2015 http://enrichmentjournal.ag.org.

_____ *Look Before You Lead: How to Discern and Shape Your Church Culture.* Grand Rapids, MI: Baker Books, 2013.

Mancini, Will. *Church Unique.* San Francisco, CA: Jossey-Bass, 2008.

Manz, Charles C. *The Leadership Wisdom of Jesus: Practical Lessons for Today.* San Francisco, CA: Berrett-Koehler Publishers, 2005.

Mayes, Jr., Eric A. *Deacon Raining in the African-American Church.* Oklahoma City, OK. B.E.A.M. Ministries Publishers, 1997.

Maxwell, John C. *The 17 Indisputable Laws of Team Work.* (Nashville, TN; Thomas

Nelson Publishers, 2013),   .

_____ *Leadership Bible.* (Nashville, TN: Thomas Nelson, Inc., 2002), 1155.

_____ Leadership 101: What Every Leader Needs to Know. Nashville, TN: Thomas Nelson, Inc., 2002.

McCollum, Dave. "The Rewards of a Deacon." *Lancaster Baptist Church.* Accessed March 3, 2015 http://www.ministry127.com.

McIntosh, Gary L. *Taking Your Church to the Next Level: What Got You Here Won't Get You There.* Grand Rapids, MI: Baker Books, 2009.

[1] McKinnon, Steve and Liz. *Interview by Ellis Armstrong*, Greensboro, NC, January 14, 2015.

McManus, Ron. "Four Qualities of Effective Leadership: Participant Note Sheet. *iTeen Challenge.* Accessed March 14, 2015 http://www.iteenchallengetraining.org/uploads/FOUR_Qualities_of_Leadership2. ppt.

McMickle, Marvin A. Deacons in Today's Black Baptist Church. Valley Forge, PA: Judson Press, 2010.

Mellowes, Marilyn. "The Black Church." *The Arthur Vining Davis Foundations: 1-7.* Accessed September 27, 2014. http:www.pbs.org/godinamerica/black-church.html.

Meyers, Joyce. *Do It Afraid!:Obeying God in the Face of Fear* (New York: Faith Words, 2008), 30.

Miller, James F. *Go Grow Your Church! Spiritual Leadership for African-American Congregations.* Cleveland, OH: The Pilgrim Press, 2008.

Minnicks, Margaret. "Changing the Method, Not the Message." *Workshop.* October 2012. Accessed April 13, 2015 http://www.examiner.com/article/minister- facilitated-the-workshop-changing-the-method-not-the-message.

Muller, Wayne. *How Then Shall We Live.* New York, NY: Bantam Books, 1997, 41.

Naylor, Robert E. *The Baptist Deacon.* Nashville, TN: B & H Books, 1998.

The New Testament Greek Lexicon Bible Dictionary. s.v. "blameless." Accessed March 14, 2015 http://www.biblestudytools.com/lexicons/greek (accessed January 6, 2015).

Newton, Gary C. *Growing Toward Spiritual Maturity.* Wheaton, IL: Crossway Books, 2004.

Palmer, Parker J. *The Courage to Teach: Exploring the Inner Landscape of a Teacher's Life*. San Francisco, CA: Jossey-Bass, 1998.

Powe, Jr., F. Douglas. *New Wine, New Wineskins*. Nashville, TN: Abingdon Press, 2012.

Priest, Christopher. The Black Church: An Outsider's Guide." *PraiseNet.Org*. March 16, 2004.   Accessed October 20, 2014. http://www.praisent.org/id11/guide/idc/

_____ "The Changing Role of the Black Church." *PraiseNet.Org*. June 17, 2007. Accessed October 20, 2014. http://www.praisenet.org/id11/center/380.hml.

Rainer, Thom S. *Autopsy of a Deceased Church*. Nashville, TN: B & H Books, 2014.

Reed, Jeff. "Church-Based Theology: Creating a New Paradigm." Presented at the BILD International Conference, Ames, Iowa on May 5, 1995. *The Paradigm Papers:1-30*. Accessed October 16, 2014. https://www.bild.org/download/paradigmPapers.pdf/html.

Robinson Jr., Joseph. *Leadership Imperatives From a Wild Man*. Valley Forge, PA: Judson Press, 2008.

Sampson, Jr., Shellie. *Superior Leadership in Challenging Situations*. Nashville, TN: Towsend Press, 1998.

Sanders, J. Oswald. *Spiritual Leadership: A Commitment to Excellence for Every Believer*. Chicago, IL: Moody, 2007. Google eBook.

Scott, John R. *The Message of Acts*. Downers Grove, IL: InterVarsity Press, 2005.

Shisko, William. "A Training Program for Deacons." *Ordained Servant*, 9, (July 2000): 62-70, Accessed February 13, 2015 http://www.opc.org/OS/html/V9/3c.html.

Searcy, Henson, and Jennifer Dykes. *Ignite*. Grand Rapids, MI: Baker Books, 2009. *Shalom Community Church*. Accessed February 16, 2015 www.http://www.shalomword.org.

Sheffield, Robert. *Deacons as Leaders*. Nashville, TN: Convention Press, 2014.

Simmons, Kim and Mike Simmons. "Visions for 21st Century Ministry Design and Community Transformation." *Power Life*. Accessed March 3, 2015. http://www.powerlife.org/Consulting/Vision.html.

"Smith-Homes Neighborhood in Greensboro, North Carolina." *City Data*. Accessed March 15, 2015. http://www.city-data.com/neighborhood/Smith-Homes-Greensboro-NC.htm.

St. James Baptist Church. *Archives.* Greensboro, NC: SJBC, 2012.

_____. *Constitution*, 2012.

Stezer, Ed and Thom S. Rainer. *Transformational Church.* Nashville, TN: B & H Books, 2010.

Stott, John. *The Message of Acts.* (Downers Grove. IL: Inter-Varsity, 1991), 56.

Strand, Robert. *In the Company of Angels.* Garden City, NY: Evergreen Press, 2005.

Strauch, Alexander. *Ministers of Mercy: The New Testament Deacon.* Littleton, CO: Lewis & Roth, 1992.

Taylor, III, Dr. James H. *Equipping Laity for Servant Leadership. Modeling a Servant's Heart, in the Rural Black Church: A Diaconate Training Resource.* Bloomington, IN: AuthorHouse, 2009.

Wagner, C. Peter. *Discover Your Spiritual Gifts.* Ventura, CA: Regal Books From Gospel Light, 2002.

Walker, John H. *A Fresh Look At the New Testament Deacon.* Lithonia, GA: Orman Press, 2001.

Ward-Turner, Kate. *Deacon Training: A Two-Part Study Guide.* Bloomington, IN: iUniverse Publisher, 2008.

Watson, Thomas. "Trees of Righteousness," *Grace Gems.* Accessed March 18, 2015 http://www.gracegems.org/watson/trees_of_righteousness.htm.

"What is on the job training (OJT)?" *Black's Law Dictionary.* Accessed March 10, 2015. www.thelawdictionary.org.

White, James Emery. *Re-thinking the Church.* Grand Rapids, MI: BakerBooks, 1997.

Wilkinson, Bruce and David Kopp. *The Dream Giver.* Sisters, Oregon: Multnomah Publishers, 2002.

_____ *A Life God Rewards.*

Wimberly, Edward P. *Recalling Our Own Stories: Spiritual Renewal for Religious Caregivers.* San Francisco: CA, Jossey-Bass, 1997.

Wuthnow, Robert. "Church Realities and Christian Identity in the 21st Century," *Religion-online. The Christian Century*, May 12, 1993, 520-523. Accessed March 18, 2015 http://www.religion-online.org/showarticles.asp?title=231.

APPENDIX A: DEACON TRAINING MODEL AT SJBC

Modules	SJBC Governance	Deacon Roles and Responsibilities	Spiritual Disciplines	Basic Ministry Skills	Deacon Partnership with the Pastor
Sermons	*Crying Over Spilled Milk*	*What the Word Will Do*	*Strength in the Journey*	*A Perfect Posture for Ministry*	*What Real Friends Will Do*
Training Agendas	Developing Vision and Mission Ordinances: Baptism Communion	Biblical Roles and Responsibilities Spiritual Qualifications of a Deacon	Prayer Fasting Giving-Spiritual Stewardship Worship	Moving Beyond Church Hurt Promoting Church Unity 5 Practices of Fruitful Congregations Visitation: Hospital and Bereavement	Roles and Responsibilities of the Pastor Establishing a Biblical Relationship with the Pastor Servant Leadership
Ministry Development	Development of a Vision and Mission Statement Restructured Communion and Baptism Services Church Wide Leadership Conferences	More Deacons as Primary Sunday School Teachers Development of a Male Usher Ministry called King's Men Media Ministry TV Broadcast	Intercessory Prayer Team Congregational Fasting Tithing Scriptures in Sunday's Bulletin Development of a Praise Team	Ministry Fair Guest Response Ministry Team Community VBS Young Adult Bible Study and Heritage Revival	Community Give Away Health Response Team Evangelism Family Care Ministry
Resources	Rethinking the Church by James Emery White Principles and Practices for Baptist Churches by Edward T. Hiscox	Now That You're A Deacon by Howard B. Foshee The Baptist Deacon by Robert E. Naylor Deacons in Today's Black Baptist Church by Marvin A. McMickle	Fasting For Spiritual Breakthrough by Elmer L. Towns Basics of Christian Faith by David Jeremiah	Deacons As Leaders by Robert Sheffield 5 Practices of Fruitful Congregations by Robert Schnase	A Fresh Look at the New Testament Deacon by Dr. John H. Walker, D. Min The Victory: Overcoming the Trials of Life by Dr. H. Norman Wright

APPENDIX B: HOUSING DEVELOPMENTS SURROUNDING SJBC

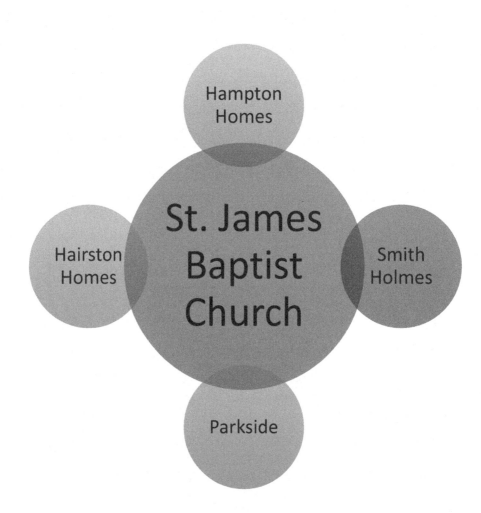

APPENDIX C: DEMOGRAPHICS OF GREENSBORO

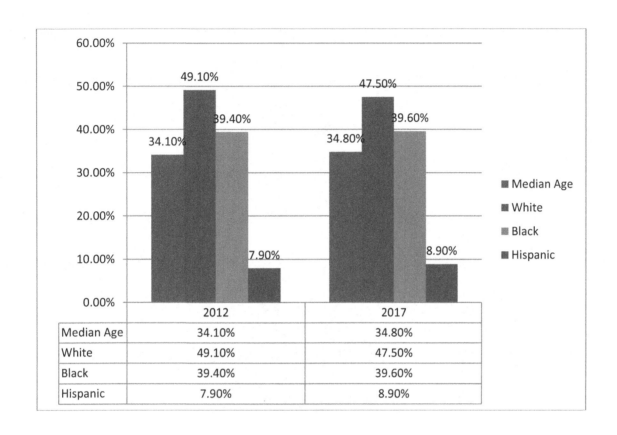

	2012	2017
Median Age	34.10%	34.80%
White	49.10%	47.50%
Black	39.40%	39.60%
Hispanic	7.90%	8.90%

**APPENDIX D: COLLEGES AND UNIVERSITITIES WITHIN A TEN MILE
RADIUS OF ST. JAMES BAPTIST CHURCH**

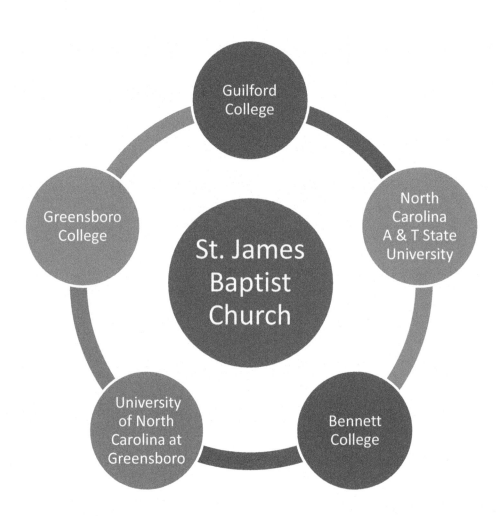

APPENDIX E: CHRISTIAN EDUCATION FOR THE DEACON

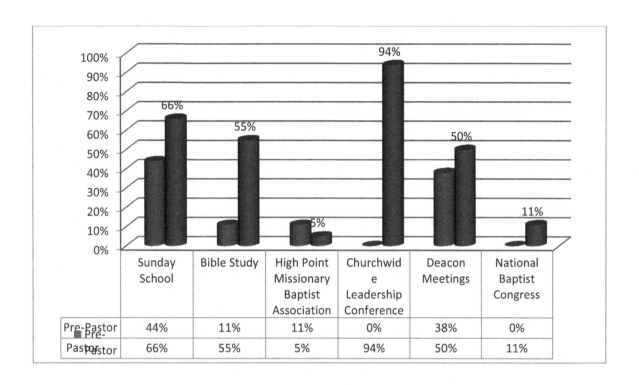

	Sunday School	Bible Study	High Point Missionary Baptist Association	Churchwide Leadership Conference	Deacon Meetings	National Baptist Congress
Pre-Pastor	44%	11%	11%	0%	38%	0%
Pastor	66%	55%	5%	94%	50%	11%

APPENDIX F: MODEL CHURCH COMPARISONS

Church	Denomination	No. of Members	Average Age of Deacons	No. of Deacons	Chair Number of Years of Service	Chairman Selection	Family Ministry
Ebenezer	Baptist	5000	51	53	4 Years	Pastor	Yes
Shalom	Non-denominational	275	45	6	3	Pastor/Elders	Yes
Love and Faith	Non-denominational	1500	50	20	10	Pastor	Yes
St. James Baptist Church	Baptist	800	60	18	18	Deacons	No

APPENDIX G: SPIRITUAL GIFTS SURVEY

LifeWay Christian Resources
2003 LifeWay Christian Resources

DIRECTIONS

This is not a test, so there are no wrong answers. The ***Spiritual Gifts Survey*** consists of 80 statements. Some items reflect concrete actions; other items are descriptive traits; and still others are statements of belief.

- Select the one response you feel best characterizes yourself and place that number in the blank provided.
- Record your answer in the blank beside each item.
- Do not spend too much time on any one item. Remember, it is not a test. Usually your
- Immediate response is best. Please give an answer for each item. Do not skip any items.
- Do not ask others how they are answering or how they think you should answer.
- Work at your own pace.

Your response choices are:

5—Highly characteristic of me/definitely true for me
4—Most of the time this would describe me/be true for me
3—Frequently characteristic of me/true for me–about 50 percent of the time
2—Occasionally characteristic of me/true for me–about 25 percent of the time
1—Not at all characteristic of me/definitely untrue for me

_____ 1. I have the ability to organize ideas, resources, time, and people effectively.
_____ 2. I am willing to study and prepare for the task of teaching.
_____ 3. I am able to relate the truths of God to specific situations.
_____ 4. I have a God-given ability to help others grow in their faith.
_____ 5. I possess a special ability to communicate the truth of salvation.
_____ 6. I have the ability to make critical decisions when necessary.
_____ 7. I am sensitive to the hurts of people.
_____ 8. I experience joy in meeting needs through sharing possessions.
_____ 9. I enjoy studying.
_____ 10. I have delivered God's message of warning and judgment.
_____ 11. I am able to sense the true motivation of persons and movements.
_____ 12. I have a special ability to trust God in difficult situations.
_____ 13. I have a strong desire to contribute to the establishment of new churches.
_____ 14. I take action to meet physical and practical needs rather than merely talking about or planning to help.
_____ 15. I enjoy entertaining guests in my home.
_____ 16. I can adapt my guidance to fit the maturity of those working with me.
_____ 17. I can delegate and assign meaningful work.

Spiritual Gifts Survey
LifeWay Christian Resources

_____ 18. I have an ability and desire to teach.
_____ 19. I am usually able to analyze a situation correctly.
_____ 20. I have a natural tendency to encourage others.
_____ 21. I am willing to take the initiative in helping other Christians grow in their faith.
_____ 22. I have an acute awareness of the emotions of other people, such as loneliness, pain, fear, and anger.
_____ 23. I am a cheerful giver.
_____ 24. I spend time digging into facts.
_____ 25. I feel that I have a message from God to deliver to others.
_____ 26. I can recognize when a person is genuine/honest.
_____ 27. I am a person of vision (a clear mental portrait of a preferable future given by God). I am able to communicate vision in such a way that others commit to making the vision a reality.
_____ 28. I am willing to yield to God's will rather than question and waver.
_____ 29. I would like to be more active in getting the gospel to people in other lands.
_____ 30. It makes me happy to do things for people in need.
_____ 31. I am successful in getting a group to do its work joyfully.
_____ 32. I am able to make strangers feel at ease.
_____ 33. I have the ability to plan learning approaches.
_____ 34. I can identify those who need encouragement.
_____ 35. I have trained Christians to be more obedient disciples of Christ.
_____ 36. I am willing to do whatever it takes to see others come to Christ.
_____ 37. I am attracted to people who are hurting.
_____ 38. I am a generous giver.
_____ 39. I am able to discover new truths.
_____ 40. I have spiritual insights from Scripture concerning issues and people that compel me to speak out.
_____ 41. I can sense when a person is acting in accord with God's will.
_____ 42. I can trust in God even when things look dark.
_____ 43. I can determine where God wants a group to go and help it get there.
_____ 44. I have a strong desire to take the gospel to places where it has never been heard.
_____ 45. I enjoy reaching out to new people in my church and community.
_____ 46. I am sensitive to the needs of people.
_____ 47. I have been able to make effective and efficient plans for accomplishing the goals of a group.
_____ 48. I often am consulted when fellow Christians are struggling to make difficult decisions.
_____ 49. I think about how I can comfort and encourage others in my congregation.

_____ 50. I am able to give spiritual direction to others.

_____ 51. I am able to present the gospel to lost persons in such a way that they accept the Lord and His salvation.

_____ 52. I possess an unusual capacity to understand the feelings of those in distress.

_____ 53. I have a strong sense of stewardship based on the recognition that God owns all things.

_____ 54. I have delivered to other persons messages that have come directly from God.

_____ 55. I can sense when a person is acting under God's leadership.

_____ 56. I try to be in God's will continually and be available for His use.

_____ 57. I feel that I should take the gospel to people who have different beliefs from me.

_____ 58. I have an acute awareness of the physical needs of others.

_____ 59. I am skilled in setting forth positive and precise steps of action.

_____ 60. I like to meet visitors at church and make them feel welcome.

_____ 61. I explain Scripture in such a way that others understand it.

_____ 62. I can usually see spiritual solutions to problems.

_____ 63. I welcome opportunities to help people who need comfort, consolation, encouragement, and counseling.

_____ 64. I feel at ease in sharing Christ with nonbelievers.

_____ 65. I can influence others to perform to their highest God-given potential.

_____ 66. I recognize the signs of stress and distress in others.

_____ 67. I desire to give generously and unpretentiously to worthwhile projects and ministries.

_____ 68. I can organize facts into meaningful relationships.

_____ 69. God gives me messages to deliver to His people.

_____ 70. I am able to sense whether people are being honest when they tell of their religious experiences.

_____ 71. I enjoy presenting the gospel to persons of other cultures and backgrounds.

_____ 72. I enjoy doing little things that help people.

_____ 73. I can give a clear, uncomplicated presentation.

_____ 74. I have been able to apply biblical truth to the specific needs of my church.

_____ 75. God has used me to encourage others to live Christlike lives.

_____ 76. I have sensed the need to help other people become more effective in their ministries.

_____ 77. I like to talk about Jesus to those who do not know Him.

_____ 78. I have the ability to make strangers feel comfortable in my home.

_____ 79. I have a wide range of study resources and know how to secure information.

_____ 80. I feel assured that a situation will change for the glory of God even when the situation seem impossible.

SCORING YOUR SURVEY

Follow these directions to figure your score for each spiritual gift.

1. Place in each box your numerical response (1-5) to the item number which is indicated below the box.
2. For each gift, add the numbers in the boxes and put the total in the TOTAL box.

LEADERSHIP	+	+	+	+	=	
Item 6	Item 16	Item 27	Item 43	Item 65		TOTAL
ADMINISTRATION	+	+	+	+	=	
Item 1	Item 17	Item 31	Item 47	Item 59		TOTAL
TEACHING	+	+	+	+	=	
Item 2	Item 18	Item 33	Item 61	Item 73		TOTAL
KNOWLEDGE	+	+	+	+	=	
Item 9	Item 24	Item 39	Item 68	Item 79		TOTAL
WISDOM	+	+	+	+	=	
Item 3	Item 19	Item 48	Item 62	Item 74		TOTAL
PROPHECY	+	+	+	+	=	
Item 10	Item 25	Item 40	Item 54	Item 69		TOTAL
DISCERNMENT	+	+	+	+	=	
Item 11	Item 26	Item 41	Item 55	Item 70		TOTAL
EXHORTATION	+	+	+	+	=	
Item 20	Item 34	Item 49	Item 63	Item 75		TOTAL
SHEPHERDING	+	+	+	+	=	
Item 4	Item 21	Item 35	Item 50	Item 76		TOTAL
FAITH	+	+	+	+	=	
Item 12	Item 28	Item 42	Item 56	Item 80		TOTAL
EVANGELISM	+	+	+	+	=	
Item 5	Item 36	Item 51	Item 64	Item 77		TOTAL
APOSTLESHIP	+	+	+	+	=	
Item 13	Item 29	Item 44	Item 57	Item 71		TOTAL
SERVICE/HELPS	+	+	+	+	=	
Item 14	Item 30	Item 46	Item 58	Item 72		TOTAL
MERCY	+	+	+	+	=	
Item 7	Item 22	Item 37	Item 52	Item 66		TOTAL
GIVING	+	+	+	+	=	
Item 8	Item 23	Item 38	Item 53	Item 67		TOTAL
HOSPITALITY	+	+	+	+	=	
Item 15	Item 32	Item 45	Item 60	Item 78		TOTAL

GRAPHING YOUR PROFILE

0
5
10
15
20
25

	SHEPHERDING
LEADERSHIP	FAITH
ADMINISTRATION	EVANGELISM
TEACHING	APOSTLESHIP
KNOWLEDGE	SERVICE/HELPS
WISDOM	MERCY
PROPHECY	GIVING
DISCERNMENT	HOSPITALITY
EXHORTATION	

1. For each gift place a mark across the bar at the point that corresponds to your TOTAL for
that gift.
2. For each gift shade the bar below the mark that you have drawn.
3. The resultant graph gives a picture of your gifts. Gifts for which the bars are tall are the ones
in which you appear to be strongest. Gifts for which the bars are very short are the ones in
which you appear not to be strong.

Now that you have completed the survey, thoughtfully answer the following questions.
The gifts I have begun to discover in my life are:
1. _____
2. _____
3. _____
    ·   After prayer and worship, I am beginning to sense that God wants me to use my spiritual gifts to serve Christ's body by
    _____.

    ·   I am not sure yet how God wants me to use my gifts to serve others. But I am committed to prayer and worship, seeking wisdom and opportunities to use the gifts I have received from God.

Ask God to help you know how He has gifted you for service and how you can begin to use this gift in ministry to others.

APPENDIX H: STAKEHOLDERS INTERVIEW QUESTIONNAIRE

1. What are the strengths of the church?

2. What are some areas, you believe, the church could improve?

3. What new ministries would you like to see?

4. What is the mission of the church?

5. What leadership roles do women occupy in the ministry?

6. What training opportunities would you like to see?

7. What training opportunities have you been a part of in the last 3 years?

APPENDIX I: DEACON PRE-ASSESSMENT

D. Min Project

Pastor Jerome Lee, Jr. M. Div.

Please take a few moments to self-reflect on the following questions and answer them to the best of your ability

1. What do you consider to be the role and responsibilities of the deacon?

2. On a scale of 1-10, (with 1 being the least and 10 being the highest), how effective are you in each of the following areas after Deacon Trainings?
    a. Problem Solving   _____
    b. Prayer Life   _____
    c. Teaching   _____
    d. Carrying out Responsibility with love and commitment   _____
    e. Maintaining confidentiality   _____
    f. Conflict Resolution   _____

3. What are you currently doing to meet the spiritual needs of the community?

4. What do you believe to be the role of the Pastor?

5. How would you describe a 21st century church?

6. What leadership roles do you see women performing in the church?

APPENDIX I: DEACON POST-ASSESSMENT

D. Min Project

Pastor Jerome Lee, Jr. M. Div.

Please take a few moments to self-reflect on the following questions and answer them to the best of your ability

1. Give an example of how you can do your work as a deacon better since the Deacon training?

2. On a scale of 1-10, **(with 1 being the least and 10 being the highest)**, how effective are you in each of the following areas after Deacon Trainings?
   - ➢ Problem Solving _____
   - ➢ Prayer Life _____
   - ➢ Teaching _____
   - ➢ Carrying out Responsibility with love and commitment _____
   - ➢ Maintaining confidentiality _____
   - ➢ Conflict Resolution _____

3. How has your understanding of the role of the deacon changed?

4. How are you now able to meet the spiritual needs of the community?

5. How has your understanding of the role of the pastor change?

6. How would you describe a 21st century church?

7. What roles do you see women playing in the 21st century church?

APPENDIX J: "TO DEACON OR NOT TO DEACON"

*This is a **survey** regarding what you believe as your role and responsibilities as a deacon and how you would prioritize their importance. If you are not a part of the Deacon's ministry, please rate what you believe are the most important responsibilities of a deacon. Rate the responsibilities from 1 (Being the most important) to 10 (Being the least important)*

Circle One: Deacon   Deaconess   Minister   Staff

A. ___Developing a spiritual growth program for the congregation

B. ___Regular and consistent attendance in Sunday school, and/or Bible Study

C. ___Supplying the pulpit in the absence of the pastor

D. ___Regular and consistent giving tithes and offerings

E. ___Conducting a Family Care Ministry

F. ___Evaluating the pastor's work

G. ___Taking communion to/visiting the members of the Healing and Recovery List

H. ___Assisting in conducting the ordinances of the church

I. ___Regular and consistent attendance in required meetings

J. ___Engaging in outreach to the un-churched (Evangelism)

K. ___Counting and lifting tithes and offering

L. ___Handling issues and concerns brought by the congregation

M. ___Daily prayer and devotion time

N. ___Supporting the pastor and the vision God has given him

O. ___Recognizing and using your spiritual gifts

APPENDIX K: ST. JAMES DEACON ROLES AND RESPONSIBILITIES
FOCUS GROUP QUESTIONS

1. Why did you agree to become a deacon?

2. What were your expectations of the role?

3. Where did you get those expectations?

4. How was the role described to you?

5. Do you recall any deacons who had an impact (positive or negative) in your life?

6. What disappointments or pleasant surprises have you encountered since becoming

   a deacon?

APPENDIX L: DEACON FAMILY CARE MINISTRY

Mission:

The mission of this ministry is to assist the pastor in meeting the physical, spiritual and emotional needs of the church member and their family. We want to make certain that every member and family in our church experiences love and support of the whole congregation. We want to be known throughout our community as a loving and caring church.

Objectives:

- To provide a clearly defined working relationship with the pastor and deacon in order that the pastoral ministries of this church be share and carried out in an orderly and effective manner that glorifies God
- To properly and adequately minister to the total physical and spiritual needs of every member of our church on a continual basis
- To create awareness on the part of the church to the total ministry of our church in order that it might bring us into a closer fellowship with one another and into the greater unity of which our Lord prayed in John 17.

Biblical Bases: Acts 6:1-7:

1   "In those days when the number of disciples was increasing, the Grecian Jews among them complained against the Hebraic Jews because their widows were being overlooked in the daily distribution of food.

2   So the Twelve gathered all the disciples together and said, "It would not be right for us to neglect the ministry of the word of God in order to wait on tables.

3   Brothers, choose seven men from among you who are known to be full of the Spirit and wisdom. We will turn this responsibility over to them

4   and will give our attention to prayer and the ministry of the word."

5   This proposal pleased the whole group. They chose Stephen, a man full of faith and of the Holy Spirit; also Philip, Procorus, Nicanor, Timon, Parmenas, and Nicolas from Antioch, a convert to Judaism.

6   They presented these men to the apostles, who prayed and laid their hands on them.

7   So the word of God spread. The number of disciples in Jerusalem increased rapidly, and a large number of priests became obedient to the faith."

Responsibilities:

- Act as the first line of communication for the members to the church
- Inform the church of needs of the family members
- Inform families of church wide events
- Contact your families throughout the year (special events, birthdays, anniversaries, etc.)
- Pray for assigned families and their needs
- Rejoice with your families to celebrate important events or accomplishments in their lives
- Lead our church families in achievement of its vision and mission
- Minister to believers and witness to unbelievers
- Demonstrate consistent stewardship through the deacon's example in tithing
- Encourage and strengthen new converts and the spiritually weak
- Provide a listening ear for their concerns and times of crisis
- Attend New Member Sunday celebration
- Make personal follow-up contact when families who are not in attendance

Plan:

This is a plan through which both deacons and associate ministers are brought together to create 7 teams. The resident church families are divided into groups based on their zip codes and assigned to a team who can minister to them.

Description:

These family assignments are:

- **Flexible** enough to allow for revision or reassignment during the course of the ministry due unforeseen situations that may arise (personal reasons, family illness, etc.)
- **Various Sizes** from assignment to assignment; Although when necessary, to keep a team from being overburdened, some other families may assigned to another deacon
- **Reassigned** every 3 years to allow the deacons opportunities to minister to all families in the church and to avoid establishing cliques that might lead to disruption or division

Encourage your families to contact you when:

- You need someone to pray for you
- You or a loved one is sick or hospitalized

- You need help in knowing and fellowshipping with other members and families
- You need Biblical advice
- You need answers to questions about your faith, denomination or church life

Ministry Teams

Wherefore, brethren, look ye out among you of honest report, full of the Holy Ghost and wisdom, whom ye may appoint over this business. But we will give ourselves continually to prayer, and to the ministry of the word." Acts 6:3-4

Teams	Deacons	Deaconess	MINISTERS	ZIP CODES
1	R. Galloway J. McClain D. Teal	L. Galloway B. McClain L. Hall	Green	27401
2	G. Swann Bobby Moore	M. Swann J. Moore Moses	Dingle Moses	27402 27403
3	J. Covington W. Hendrix	B. Hendrix M. Keck E. Goode Mother Thomas	Bennett T. Williams	27407
4	G. Gillis T. Williams	D. Gillis R. Williams M. Smith C. Lee	Rankin Walker	27406
5	E. Armstrong J. Courts A. Ross	B. Armstrong H. Courts H. Ross C. Emerson V. McKnight	McKnight	27408 27410
6	H. Bryant Brian Moore Z. Sharpe	R. Bryant R. Moore A. Sharpe	Alston	27405 27455
7	W. Johnson C. Miller P. Haizlip	P. Johnson E. Miller M. Harris	Burton, J. Williams	27301 27214 27215 *Other Outside Zip Codes

APPENDIX M: MODULE TRAINING AGENDAS

- **M1:** **Governance** (7 Training Agendas/Lesson Plans)

- **M2:** **Deacon Roles and Responsibilities** (8 Training Agendas/Lesson Plans)

- **M3:** **Spiritual Disciplines** (10 Training Agendas/Lesson Plans)

- **M4:** **Basic Ministry Skills** (16 Training Agendas/Lesson Plans)

- **M5:** **Deacon Partnership With the Pastor** (5 Training Agendas/Lesson Plans)

APPENDIX M 1

MODULE 1: GOVERNANCE

Session 1:   Vision and Mission *(Part 1)*

Session 2:   Vision and Mission *(Part 2)*

Session 3:   Vision and Mission *(Part 3)*

Session 4:   Vision and Mission *(Part 4)*

Session 5:   Baptism

Session 6:   Communion

Session 7:   Baptism and Communion Review

        • Handouts A, B, C

SJBC CHURCH-WIDE LEADERSHIP CONFERENCE AGENDA

Facilitators: Pastor Jerome Lee, Jr. M.Div. and Dr. Dwight Riddick

Module:	Governance
Session 1:	Vision and Mission *(Part 1)*
Audience:	Church wide Leadership
Time Frame:	**Friday, 7:00 pm-9:00pm** and Saturday, 9:00 am-12:00 noon
Guiding Scripture:	*"So built we the wall; and all the wall was joined together unto the half thereof: for the people had a work. Nehemiah 4:6 KJV*
Resources Used:	Ten Leadership Lessons from Nehemiah by Lovett H. Weems, Jr. How to Bring Your Church New Strength by Dr. Richard J. Krejcir;

7:00   Devotionals

7:15   Greetings and Overview

Objectives: *At the end of this session, the participant will:*

- Know the role of Pastor and leaders in God's vision for His people
- Understand where the vision comes from and how it operates in the body of Christ
- Understand the need to work in unity with enthusiasm and positivity

7:25   **Activities:**   Ask the participants to tell you what the word *vision* means to them and then ask them to give some words opposite to the meaning.

Next Blindfold one of the participants and put some obstacles in their path and have them walk to a certain destination to show the difficulty in attempting to go somewhere without seeing where we are going.

7:35   **Lesson I:** How to Bring your Church New Strength
- Rediscover your purpose
- Return to the Original Vision
- Rededicate the Church Family
- Reorganize Your Approach to the Community
- Remember

SJBC Church-Wide Leadership Conference Agenda

Facilitators: Pastor Jerome Lee, Jr. M.Div. and Dr. Dwight Riddick

Module:	Governance
Session 2:	Vision and Mission *(Part 2)*
Audience:	Church wide Leadership
Time Frame:	**Friday, 7:00 pm-9:00pm** and Saturday, 9:00 am-12:00 noon
Guiding Scripture:	*"So built we the wall; and all the wall was joined together unto the half thereof: for the people had a work. Nehemiah 4:6 KJV*
Resources Used:	Ten Leadership Lessons from Nehemiah by Lovett H. Weems, Jr. How to Bring Your Church New Strength by Dr. Richard J. Krejcir;

7:50   **Lesson II:** God's Vision and Nehemiah's Leadership Example
- Response of the Leader
- Care for the people
- Clarity in direction and vision
- Team building
- Prayer is essential
- God's vision is simple
- The Leader keeps the real purpose before the people
- Handling adversity
- Another vision

8:05   **Lesson III:** The Church Leader Mandate (excerpt from the book 21st Century Strategies for Church Growth)

8:15   **Lesson IV:** Healthy and Unhealthy Churches

8:30   Q/A

8:55   Closing Prayer

SJBC Church-Wide Leadership Conference Agenda

Facilitators: Pastor Jerome Lee, Jr. M.Div. and Dr. Dwight Riddick

Module:	Governance
Session 3:	Vision and Mission *(Part 3)*
Audience:	Church wide Leadership
Time Frame:	Friday, 7:00 pm-9:00pm and **Saturday, 9:00 am-12:00 noon**
Guiding Scripture:	*"So built we the wall; and all the wall was joined together unto the half thereof: for the people had a work. Nehemiah 4:6 KJV*
Resources Used:	Ten Leadership Lessons from Nehemiah by Lovett H. Weems, Jr. How to Bring Your Church New Strength by Dr. Richard J. Krejcir;

9:00   Continental Breakfast

9:45   Devotionals

10:00   Greetings and Overview

Objectives: *At the end of this session, the participant will:*

- Understand the meaning of vision
- Understand the importance of vision
- Trust God for provision for the vision
- Submit to God for the vision

10:10   **Review:** Session I: Vision and Mission-Nehemiah's Leadership Example (The Facilitator will ask the participants to tell what vision means as discussed in the first session and to name some leadership lessons from Nehemiah's example)

10:25   **Lesson 1: The importance of a vision**
- People will not perish   Proverbs

  29:18

- People will grow spiritually and be fulfilled Habakkuk 2:2-

  3

- People must hear and know God's word   Romans 10:14-15

- People must know God and believe Him   Hebrews 11:16

SJBC CHURCHWIDE LEADERSHIP CONFERENCE AGENDA

Facilitators: Pastor Jerome Lee, Jr. M.Div. and Dr. Dwight Riddick

Module:	Governance
Session 4:	Vision and Mission *(Part 4)*
Audience:	Church wide Leadership
Time Frame:	Friday, 7:00 pm-9:00pm and **Saturday, 9:00 am-12:00 noon**
Guiding Scripture:	*"So built we the wall; and all the wall was joined together unto the half thereof: for the people had a work. Nehemiah 4:6 KJV*
Resources Used:	Ten Leadership Lessons from Nehemiah by Lovett H. Weems, Jr. How to Bring Your Church New Strength by Dr. Richard J. Krejcir;

11:00   **Break……………………………………………..10 minutes**

11:10   **Lesson 2: Understanding vision**
- God provides, preserves and protects the vision……..Genesis 22

11:25   **Lesson 3: Place of vision**
- Walking in obedience leads us where God want us…Genesis 22:9

11:40   **Lesson 4: Submission to the vision**
- Brings provision for the vision……………………Genesis 22:7-8

- He will supply our every need
  (provision)………Philippians 4:19
- He will direct us if we trust him…………………..Proverbs
  3:5-6

11:50   Discussion and Q/A

12:00   Closing Prayer

12:15   **Lunch**

SJBC WEEKLY BIBLE STUDY AGENDA

Facilitator: Pastor Jerome Lee, Jr. M.Div.

Module:	SJBC Governance
Session 5:	Baptism
Audience:	Bible Study Participants
Time Frame:	Tuesday @ 7pm and Wednesday @12 noon
Guiding Scripture:	*"One Lord, one faith, and one baptism" Ephesians 4:5*
Resources Used:	**www.middletownbiblechurch.org /,**

6:45   Devotionals

7:00   Greetings and Overview

Review of Objectives   *At the end of this session, the participant will:*

- Be able to explain what the word baptism means
- Be able to discuss the 3 different methods churches use to baptize
- Be able to interpret and discuss scripture that address baptism

7:15   Lesson 1: Baptism

Activity: The facilitator will break up participants into groups of 6; On and 8x11 sheet of paper make a Web. In the center, place the word "baptism". From the center circle draw lines describing your understanding of baptism.

7:30   Share out their charts with the whole group.

7:40   Lecture: Questions to be addressed: (Have participants remained in same
groups)

1. What does the word baptism mean?
2. What is the method that we as Baptists use?
3. Does water baptism save a person?

Activity: Scripture Search of: Matthew 28:19, Acts 8:36-39; John 3:23 and Acts 16:31 (Have each group to answer the questions using the scriptures).

8:00   Discuss answers to questions

8:25   **Activity:** Pass out scriptures already printed on a sheet of paper: John 3:16, John 6:47, Acts 10:43, Acts 16:31 and 1Corinthians 1:21. Read them carefully and line out the part that is incorrect and not found in the Bible. Discus after 15 minutes.

8:50   Closing Prayer

SJBC WEEKLY BIBLE STUDY AGENDA

Facilitator: Pastor Jerome Lee, Jr. M.Div.

Module:	SJBC Governance
Session 6:	Communion
Audience:	Deacons and Deaconesses
Time Frame:	Tuesday @ 7pm and Wednesday @12 noon
Guiding Scripture:	*"This is my body which is for you; do this in remembrance of me." 1 Cor. 11:24*
Resources Used:	www.middletownbiblechurch.org; /www.christianity.com/church/church..../

6:45   Devotionals

7:00   Greetings and Overview

Review of Objectives   *At the end of this session, the participant will:*

- Be able to explain what the meaning of the word "communion"
- Be able to discuss the 5 different names given for the act of communion
- Be able to identify who should participate in the communion service

7:10   Lesson 2: **Activity:** In groups of 5 to 6 people, create a KWL chart. In this chart fill in what you already know about communion and what you would like to know. Share out from their chart their understanding of what communion means

7:25   **Lecture**:
1) Discuss the actual meaning of communion
2) What are the 5 different names given to the acts of communion?
3) Discuss who should participate in communion.
4) Understand the challenges in giving communion to often or not often enough

8:25   **Activity:** In your same group, have the participants to complete the "L" portion of their chart (What they have learned about communion). Discuss what they have learned.

8:35   Discus the Challenges in giving communion to often or not enough

1. Challenge with giving communion too often
2. Challenge with giving communion not enough

8:55   Closing Prayer

SJBC WEEKLY BIBLE STUDY AGENDA

Facilitator: Pastor Jerome Lee, Jr. M.Div.

Module:	SJBC Governance
Session 7:	Baptism and Communion Review
Audience:	Bible Study Participants
Time Frame:	Tuesday @ 7pm and Wednesday @12 noon
Guiding Scripture:	*"One Lord, one faith, and one baptism" Ephesians 4:5*
Resources Used:	www.middletownbiblechurch.org /, www.christianity.com/church/church..../

6:45   Devotionals

7:00   Greetings and Overview

Review of Objectives   *At the end of this session, the participant will:*

- Be able to explain what both baptism and communion means
- Be able to compare and contrast baptism and communion

7:10   **Activity 1:** Review Baptism (Pass out Handout A: have each participant to complete individually.)

7:25   Share out answers from Handout A with the group.

7:35   **Activity 2**: Review Communion (Pass out Handout B: have each participant to complete individually)

7:55   Share out answers from Handout B with the group.

8:05   **New Learning:** The 4 LOOKS of Communion

8:20   **Activity 3:** Compare/Contrast the 2 ordinances of the church: Baptism and Communion (*The participants will be given Handout C to fill in as the facilitator reviews the 2 ordinances*).

8:30   Have the entire group to read together: Matthew 28:18-20; and 1 Corinthians 11:23-34

8:40   Look back at Handout C on What to Remember on Baptism and Communion

8:50   Closing Prayer

HANDOUT A: BAPTISM

1) Read Acts 2:41; Acts 10:43-48 and Acts 16:30-34. After reading and thinking about these verses, number the following according to the correct order:

_____ They were baptized.

_____ They were saved.

_____ They heard God's Word (they heard the gospel).

_____ They believed on Christ.

Baptism is not something that a person does to be saved; baptism is something that a saved person does.

2) Write TRUE or FALSE for the following:

_____ "I want to be baptized in water so that I can be saved."

_____ "I want to be baptized in water because I am saved."

_____ "When I am baptized in water my sins will be all washed away."

_____ The moment I believed in Christ all my sins were washed away and forgiven." See Acts 10:43.

_____ Baptism is not something that unsaved people should do; baptism is something that saved people should do."

3) Explain the picture below:

HANDOUT B: **COMMUNION**

A. **Using your notes, write the 5 names given for communion:**

1._____

2._____

3._____

4._____

5._____

B. **What does Communion Picture?**

Like Baptism, Communion presents a very important picture. The bread is a symbol (a picture) of _____ (Matthew 26:26) and the cup is a symbol (a picture) of _____ (Matthew 26:27-28). What did Jesus mean when He said, "**This is My Body**" and "**This is My blood**"? There are churches today that believe that the Communion bread actually changes and becomes the body of Christ. They believe also that the juice of the grape actually changes and becomes the blood of Jesus.

C. **New learning:** The 4 "LOOKS" pertaining Communion *(To be completed with the facilitator)*

 a. **BACKWARD LOOK**—looking back to the cross to see and to remember what the Lord Jesus has done for me by the offering up of His body and the shedding of His precious blood (1 Peter 1:18-19; 2:24; 3:18; 2 Corinthians 5:21; Ephesians 1:7; Matthew 26:28).

 b. **AN UPWARD LOOK**—looking unto Jesus who is presently doing a work for me as my **Intercessor** (Hebrews 7:25; Romans 8:34) and **Advocate** (1 John 2:1-2), having sat down at the right hand of the Father (Hebrews 1:3; 8:1).

 c. **A FORWARD LOOK**—looking for Jesus (Titus 2:13) and expecting and waiting (1 Corinthians 1:7-8) for what He will do as He comes again to complete the great work of salvation which He began in me (Philippians 1:6; 3:20-21). Paul said that when believers partake of Communion they are showing (proclaiming) the Lord's death till He _____ (1 Corinthians 11:26). Thus Communion looks back to the cross and looks ahead to His coming again.

 d. **AN INWARD LOOK**—looking at what Jesus is doing in me (1 Cor. 11:27-32; Phil. 2:13). The believer must "E_____ himself" (1 Corinthians 11:28). This means that I must put myself to the test. I must examine myself to make sure my heart is right with the Lord.

HANDOUT C: BAPTISM AND COMMUNION—A COMPARISON

WATER BAPTISM	COMMUNION
Done only _____	Done _____ times
Done at the _____ of the Christian life	Done _____ the Christian life
Key Word: _____ (identification) See Romans 6:3-4. The believer is identified with Jesus Christ.	Key Word: _____ (fellowship) See 1 Corinthians 10:16; 11:28,31. The believer is able to fellowship with Jesus Christ.
Because of the cross I have a new life!	Because of the cross I can enjoy the new life that I have!
I am a new creature in Christ!	I need to walk as a new creature in Christ!
My _____ (POSITION) in Christ is perfect! God sees me in His perfect Son!	My actual _____ is not always what it should be. I need to "examine myself" and "judge myself" to make sure that I come to God through the cross and stay in fellowship with Him (1 Cor. 11:28-32; 1 John 1:5-9).

The next time you witness a Baptism service remember:
1. When you were outside of Christ
2. When you accepted Christ as your Savior
3. When you were baptized in Christ

The next time you take Communion you can think about these four "looks":

1) A BACKWARD LOOK--"Thank You Lord for what You did for me on the cross."

2) AN UPWARD LOOK--"Thank You Lord that You are my Savior, my Lord, my Helper, and my Keeper right now."

3) A FORWARD LOOK--"Thank You Lord that you are coming again, perhaps even today."

4) AN INWARD LOOK--"Thank You Lord that if I confess my sins, You are faithful and just to forgive my sins and cleanse.

APPENDIX M 2

MODULE 2: DEACON ROLES AND RESPONSIBILITIES

Session 1:   A Theology of Deacons

Session 2:   Deacon Qualifications

Session 3:   The Practice of Deacons (Part 1)

Session 4:   The Practice of Deacons (Part 2)

Session 5:   Understanding the Role of the Pastor (Part 1)

Session 6:   Understanding the Role of the Pastor (Part 2)

Session 7:   Deacon Relationships

Session 8:   Understanding the Role of the Deaconess

SJBC Deacon/Deaconess Training Agenda

Facilitator: Pastor Jerome Lee, Jr. M.Div.

Module:	Deacon Roles and Responsibilities
Session 1:	The Biblical Role of Deacons: A Theology of Deacons
Audience:	Deacons and Deaconesses
Time Frame:	Saturday @ 10a.m-12:00 noon and **2nd & 4th Thursday @ 6:30-8:30 pm**
Guiding Scripture:	*"Men of good reputation, full of the Holy Spirit and wisdom."- Act 6:3*
Resources Used:	www.baptiststart.com/path_to_leadership/deacon_roles

6:20   Devotionals

6:30   Greetings and Overview

Review of Objectives: *(At the end of the session, the participants will)*

- Be able to understand the original purpose of Deacons
- Be able explore the Spiritual and Moral Qualifications of a Deacon

6:40   **Lesson 1:** The Biblical Role of Deacons

Activity: *(Break into small groups of three.)* Discuss: "What is the role of the deacon at SJBC? *(The participants will share in small groups for 10 minutes and then share out with whole group.*

7:00   **Lecture:** Questions to be addressed:

- Why there is a need for the deacon?
- What was the original purpose for the deacon?
- What are the core qualifications of a deacon?

7:50   **Lesson 2:** Explore the Spiritual and Moral Qualifications of a Deacon

Spiritual Qualifications: (Acts 6:1-6) 1. Full of the Holy Spirit; 2. Full of Wisdom; 3. Full of Faith
  Moral Qualifications: (1 Timothy 3:8-10, 12-13) 1. Worthy of Respect; 2. Sincere; 3. Not
    indulging in much wine; 4. Not pursuing dishonest gain; 5. The husband of one wife; 6.
    Manages his children and household well;

8:15   Discussion and Q/A

8:25   Closing Prayer

SJBC Deacon/Deaconess Training Agenda

Facilitator: Pastor Jerome Lee, Jr. M.Div.

Module:	Deacon Roles and Responsibilities
Session 2:	The Biblical Role of Deacons: Deacon Qualifications
Audience:	Deacons and Deaconesses
Time Frame:	Saturday @ 10a.m-12:00 noon and **2nd & 4th Thursday @ 6:30-8:30 pm**
Guiding Scripture:	*"In the same way, deacons are to be worthy of respect, sincere, not indulging in much wine, and not pursuing dishonest gain." 1 Timothy 3:8-13*
Resources Used:	*The Baptist Deacon, by Robert E. Naylor* (Chapter 2: Qualifications of a Deacon)

6:20   Devotionals

6:30   Greetings and Overview
Review of Objective (*At the end of this session, the participants will :*)
Be able to review the spiritual and moral qualifications of a deacon
Be able to identify qualifications in Acts 6: The Pattern of the Seven
Be able to identify qualifications in 1 Timothy 3

6:40   **Lecture:** *(Examine qualifications in Acts 6)*
Honest report
Full of the Holy Ghost
Full of Faith
Business men

7:40   **Lecture**: (*Examine qualifications in 1 Timothy 3)*
Not doubled tongued
Not given to much wine
Not greedy of filthy lucre
Grave
Holding the mystery of faith
Proved
Being blameless
Husband of one wife

8:20   Questions and Answers

8:30   Closing Prayer

SJBC Deacon/Deaconess Training Agenda

Facilitator: Pastor Jerome Lee, Jr. M.Div.

Module:	Deacon Roles and Responsibilities
Session 3:	The Biblical Role of Deacons: *The Practice of Deacons (Part 1)*
Audience:	Deacons and Deaconesses
Time Frame:	Saturday @ 10a.m-12:00 noon and **2nd & 4th Thursday @ 6:30-8:30 pm**
Guiding Scripture:	*"Paul and Timothy, servants of Christ Jesus: to all the saints in Christ Jesus who are at Philippi, including the overseers and deacons." – Philippians 1:1*
Resources Used:	www.baptiststart.com/path_to_leadership/deacon_roles

6:20   Devotionals

6:30   Greetings and Overview

Review of Objectives: *(At the end of this session, the participants will)*

- Be able to review what it means to be a deacon according to scripture
- Be able to understand the 2 main areas of service for deacons

6:40   **Activity:** Ask each participant to write 5-8 sentences as to what it means to be a deacon according to scripture and using their notes from last week's training.

6:55   Have participants to share out (10 minutes).

7:05   **Pose the question**: "How does a deacon know what to do?" Discuss the pros and cons of these ways listed below. (Turn and Talk) and Share out

- He makes a guess!
- He follows tradition!
- He learns on the job!
- He follows other deacons!

7:30   **Lecture:** There are 2 main areas of service for a deacon:

- Community Focused
- Mission Focused

8:30   Have participants get into groups of 4 and pray for the needs of the congregation and how they can be a part of meeting their needs through service.

8:45   Closing Prayer

SBJC Monthly Saturday Training Agenda

Facilitator: Pastor Jerome Lee, Jr. M.Div.

Module:	Deacon Roles and Responsibilities
Session 4:	The Biblical Role of Deacons: The Practice of Deacons *(Part 2)*
Audience:	Deacons and Deaconesses
Time Frame: pm	**Saturday @ 10a.m-12:00 noon** and 2nd & 4th Thursday @ 6:30-8:30
Guiding Scripture:	*"They first must be tested and then if there is nothing against them, let them serve as deacons; 1 Timothy 3:10*
Resources Used:	National Ministries – McDonald Jackson

9:50   Devotionals

10:00   Greetings and Overview: At the end of this session, the participants will:
- Review Biblical background
- Explore Opportunities for service
- Functions of the Diaconate

10:15   Lesson 1: Biblical background

Activity: Discussion: "Why did you agree to become a deacon?" Discuss with the group.

10:35   Lecture: Questions to be addressed:

- Biblical background of the Diaconate ministries (1Timothy 3)
- Challenges that keep deacon boards from servant leadership?
- Servant leadership training opportunities.

11:00 **Break..10 minutes**

11:10 Lesson 2: Functions of the Diaconate ministry

- Ordinances: helping with baptism and Lord's Supper
- Worship: working with the pastor in the worship service
- Spiritual development and care of church members
- Outreach: caring for those in need in the church community, and the world, and addressing social concerns.

11:45 Discussion and Q/A

11:55 Closing Prayer

SJBC Deacon/Deaconess Training Agenda

Facilitator: Pastor Jerome Lee, Jr. M.Div.

Module:	Deacon Roles and Responsibilities
Session 5:	The Biblical Role of Deacons: *Understanding the role of the Pastor (Part 1)*
Audience:	Deacons and Deaconesses
Time Frame:	Saturday @ 10a.m-12:00 noon and **2nd & 4th Thursday @ 6:30-8:30 pm**
Guiding Scripture:	*"Paul and Timothy, servants of Christ Jesus: to all the saints in Christ Jesus who are at Philippi, including the overseers and deacons." – Philippians 1:1*
Resources Used:	www.baptiststart.com/path_to_leadership/deacon_roles

6:20   Devotionals

6:30   Greetings and Overview

Review of Objectives: (At the end of this session, the participants will):
- Be able to understand overseers are not deacons and deacons are not overseers
- Be able to recognize evidences Deacons are acting as a Board

6:40   **Lesson 1:** The Pastor is the Shepherd

Activity: Group discussion: Ways a Good Shepherd leads the flock.

7:00   **Lecture:** Questions to be addressed:

- What is an Elder?
- How should shepherds lead the flock?

7:45   **Lesson 2:** Evidences Deacons Are Acting as a Board

- **Screening:** When all major recommendations from church operations and church committees are screened by the deacons
- **Personnel:** When the pastor and staff members are directly responsible to the deacons rather than to the church.
- **Finances:** When the use or expenditure of major church resources, such as facilities and finances, must first be approved by the deacons.

8:15   Discussion and Q/A

8:25   Closing Prayer

SJBC Deacon/Deaconess Training Agenda

Facilitator: Pastor Jerome Lee, Jr. M.Div.

Module:	Deacon Roles and Responsibilities
Session 6:	The Biblical Role of Deacons: *Understanding the role of the Pastor (Part 2)*
Audience:	Deacons and Deaconesses
Time Frame:	Saturday @ 10a.m-12:00 noon and **2nd & 4th Thursday @ 6:30-8:30 pm**
Guiding Scripture:	*"And I will give you pastors according to mine heart, who will feed you with knowledge and understanding."-Jeremiah 3:15*
Resources Used:	*Shepherding the Sheep* by Dr. Benjamin S. Baker/Understanding Your Pastor

6:20   Devotionals

6:30   Greetings and Overview
Review of Objective: (*At the end of this session, the participants will*):

- Be able to understand the roles and responsibility of the Pastor
- Be able to identify the Four Pastoral Models
- Be able to identify Seven Shepherd Models

6:40   **Lesson 1:** The Four Pastoral Models
Activity: Expectations of a Pastor – Questionnaire (handout). Self-reflection.

7:00   Lecture: Questions to be addressed:

Preaching roles?   Healing responsibilities
Teaching duties?   Praying responsibilities

7:30   **Lesson 2:** Seven Shepherd Models

1. Shepherd –Matthew 4:23   5. Enabler – Ephesian 4:11-12

2. Overseer - Acts 20:28   6. Administrator – 1Corinthians   9:19,22

3. Supervisor – Matt. 10:1-8   7. Counselor – Isaiah 1:18

4. Organizer – Ex 18:17-23

8:00   Questions and Answers

8:25   Closing Prayer

SJBC Deacon/Deaconess Agenda

Facilitator: Pastor Jerome Lee, Jr. M.Div.

Module:	Deacon Roles and Responsibilities
Session 7:	The Biblical Role of Deacons: *Deacon Relationships*
Audience:	Deacons and Deaconesses
Time Frame:	Saturday @ 10a.m-12:00 noon and **2nd & 4th Thursday @ 6:30-8:30 pm**
Guiding Scripture:	*"In the same way, deacons are to be worthy of respect, sincere, not indulging in much wine, and not pursuing dishonest gain." 1 Timothy 3:8-13*
Resources Used:	*http://www.sermonnotebook.org/new*

6:20   Devotionals

6:30   Greetings and Overview
          Review of Objective *(At the end of this session, the participants will):*

- Be able to understand the 4 basic relationships of Deacons
  - A Deacon's relationship to the **Savior**
  - A Deacon's relationship to the **Spiri**t
  - A Deacon's relationship to the **Shepherd**
  - A Deacon's relationship to the **Saints**

6:40   **Activity:** Divide participants into 4 groups. Assign each group a specific relationship and on chart paper, describe what that relationship would look like. Have each group to present their chart.

7:15   **Lecture and Discussion:** *(Examine Acts 6:1-7)*

- His relationship with the Savior *(also look at 1 Timothy 3:8-13)*
- His relationship with the Spirit *(Ephesians 5:18, Galatians 5:22-23, John 16:13, 1 Corinthians 12:13, and Romans 8:9)*
- His relationship with the Shepherd *(Ephesians 5:23, Hebrews 13:7, 17)*
- His relationships with the Saints *(John 5:19-20; 1 Timothy 3:13)*

8:15   Summarize information learned by going back to their initial group charts and add information that they may have been missing.

8:30   Closing Prayer

SJBC Deacon/Deaconess Agenda

Facilitator: Pastor Jerome Lee, Jr. M.Div.

Module:	Deacon Roles and Responsibilities
Session 9:	The Biblical Role of Deacons: Understanding the role of the Deaconess
Audience:	Deacons and Deaconesses
Time Frame:	Saturday @ 10a.m-12:00 noon and **2nd & 4th Thursday @ 6:30-8:30 pm**
Guiding Scripture:	*"Whosoever wants to be first, must be last of all and servant of all." Mark 9:35*
Resources Used:	http://www.sermonnotebook.org/new

6:20   Devotionals

6:30   Greetings and Overview

Review of Objective: *(At the end of this session, the participants will)*

- Be able to understand Deaconess qualifications
- Be able to explore role for Deaconess in "todays" church

6:40   **Lesson 1:** Preacher and deacon similarities

Activity: Turn and talk to your neighbor: "Do you think the role of the deaconess meet the needs of the church?" Discuss with the group.

7:20   **Lecture:** Questions to be addressed:

- Appointment of a Deaconess
- Is the position of deaconess scriptural? (Romans 16:1)
- Is the position mandatory (Mark 7:6)

7:50   **Lesson 2:** Explore role for Deaconess in 'today's' church

- Deacon/Deaconess transferring church membership
- Deacon's Beatitude
- Role of Deacon/deaconess in "todays" church

8:15   Discussion and Q/A

8:25   Closing Prayer

APPENDIX M 3

MODULE 3: SPIRITUAL DISCIPLINES

Session 1:   Prayer *(Part 1)*

               Handout A

Session 2:   Prayer *(Part 2)*

Session 3:   Fasting *(Part 1)*

Session 4:   Fasting *(Part 2)*

Session 5:   Biblical Stewardship: Preparing for Growth and Harvest *(Part 1)*

Session 6:   Biblical Stewardship: Preparing for Growth and Harvest *(Part 2)*

Session 7:   Biblical Stewardship: Preparing for Growth and Harvest *(Part 3)*

Session 8:   Biblical Stewardship: Preparing for Growth and Harvest *(Part 4)*

Session 9:   What is true worship?

Session 10:   Worship in the Old Testament

SJBC Weekly Bible Study Agenda

Facilitator: Pastor Jerome Lee, Jr. M.Div.

Module:	Spiritual Disciplines
Session 1:	Prayer *(Part 1)*
Audience:	Bible Study Participants
Time Frame:	Tuesday @ 7pm and Wednesday @12 noon
Guiding Scripture:	*"And pray in the Spirit on all occasions with all kinds of prayers and requests."* *Eph.6:18 NIV*
Resources Used:	*Fasting for Spiritual Break Through by Elmer L. Towns*

6:45   Devotionals

7:00   Greetings and Review of Objectives

- To understand the uniqueness of prayer
- To cite scripture passages relevant to the practice of prayer
- To discover God's responsiveness to us according to His divine purpose.

7:10   **Activity:** (attached):   Handout A: **AGREE/DISAGREE:**

As a volunteer reads each statement, raise your hand to indicate whether you AGREE (open hand) or whether you DISAGREE (closed fist).

7:20   **Lesson 1: "Insights into the Practice of Prayer"**

8:20   **Activity:** Circle or highlight three (3) key principles from the lesson that gave insight into your practice of prayer.

8:30   Share out Discussion: Share your response to one of the reflection points located at the end of this lesson.

8:40   Review / Summary

8:50   Closing Prayer

Handout A: Agree/Disagree

As a volunteer reads each statement, raise your hand to indicate whether you AGREE (open hand) or whether you DISAGREE (closed fist).

1. Prayers should be said aloud.

2. Prayer changes us inwardly.

3. There is no connection between prayer and meditation.

4. The best way to learn to pray is to imitate what we see an hear others do.

5. Corporate or group prayers are unscriptural.

6. God hears all prayers.

7. Complaining to God should be avoided when praying.

SJBC Weekly Bible Study Agenda

Facilitator: Pastor Jerome Lee, Jr. M.Div.

Module:	Spiritual Disciplines
Session 2:	Prayer *(Part 2)*
Audience:	Bible Study Participants
Time Frame:	Tuesday @ 7pm and Wednesday @12 noon
Guiding Scripture: *Eph.6:18 NIV*	*"And pray in the Spirit on all occasions with all kinds of prayers and requests."*
Resources Used:	*Fasting for Spiritual Break Through by Elmer L. Towns*

6:45   Devotionals

7:00   Greetings and Review of Objectives

- To define prayer as a Spiritual Discipline
- To understand the believer's need for prayer

7:10   **Activity:** BRAINSTORM: Work with a partner to list various areas of life that require discipline. (*List as many things as possible within five minutes.*)

7:20   **Lesson 2: "Prayer: A Practice of Inward Discipline"**

8:20   **Activity:** REFLECT: Write your personal response(s) to the "reflection points located at the end of the lesson.

8:30   Share out/ Discussion: Volunteers share one response with the whole group.

8:40   Review / Summary

8:50   Closing Prayer

SJBC Weekly Bible Study Agenda

Facilitator: Pastor Jerome Lee, Jr. M.Div.

Module:	Spiritual Disciplines
Session 3:	Fasting *(Part 1)*
Audience:	Bible Study Participants
Time Frame:	Tuesday @ 7pm and Wednesday @12 noon
Guiding Scripture: *Eph.6:18 NIV*	*"And pray in the Spirit on all occasions with all kinds of prayers and requests."*
Resources Used:	*Celebration of Discipline by Richard Foster*

6:45   Devotionals

7:00   Greetings and Review of Objectives

- To define fasting as a spiritual discipline
- To understand the need for fasting
- To consider incorporating fasting as a discipline into your life.

7:10   **Activity:** REMEMBER WHEN:

Volunteers speak to the group to recount a time when they fasted and experienced the outcome of the fast.

7:20   **Lesson 3:** "Fasting as a Spiritual Discipline"

8:20   **Activity:** IF…. THEN …STATEMENT

Complete this statement: If I fasted about _____. Then, the ending might be _____

8:30   Share out Discussion: Share your IF/THEN statement with 3-4 people seated near you.

8:40   Review / Summary

8:50   Closing Prayer

SJBC Weekly Bible Study Agenda

Facilitator: Pastor Jerome Lee, Jr. M.Div.

Module:	Spiritual Disciplines
Session 4:	Fasting *(Part 2)*
Audience:	Bible Study Participants
Time Frame:	Tuesday @ 7pm and Wednesday @12 noon
Guiding Scripture: Eph.6:18 NIV	*"And pray in the Spirit on all occasions with all kinds of prayers and requests."*
Resources Used:	*Celebration of Discipline by Richard Foster*

6:50   Devotionals

7:00   Greetings and Review of Objectives

- To make connection between fasting and prayer
- To recognize the purpose of various types of fasting.

7:10   **Activity** (attached): SCAVENGER HUNT

Search your Bible for a short passage or verse about each of the following people: (1)Elijah; (2) Ezra; (3) The disciples; 4: The poor widow of Zarephath. Share your findings with those seated next to you.

7:20   **Lesson 4:** (This lesson may be taught in four parts)

"Prayer and Fasting: Incorporating Fasting into Your Life"

8:20   **Activity**: ONE SENTENCE SUMMARY

In a single sentence, write a summary of this lesson.

8:30   Share out Discussion: How does fasting as you studied it in this lesson, differ for others you have used or heard of?

8:40   Review / Summary

8:50   Closing Prayer

SBJC Monthly Saturday Training Agenda

Facilitator: Pastor Jerome Lee, Jr. M.Div.

Module: `	Spiritual Disciplines
Session 5:	Biblical Stewardship: Preparing for Growth and Harvest *(Part 1)*
Audience:	Church Wide
Time Frame:	Saturday @ 10a.m-12:00 noon
Guiding Scripture:	*"To everything there is a season and a time to every purpose under the heaven," Ecclesiastes 3:1*
Resources Used:	*Celebration of Discipline by Richard Foster*

9:50   Devotionals

10:00   Greetings and Overview

Review of Objectives   *At the end of this session, the participant will:*

- Be able to identify and recognize the church as a business.
- Be able understand the importance of managing money.
- Realize we are honoring God through money and ministry.

10:15   **Lesson 1:** Preparing for Growth and Harvest: The Church as a Business

Activity: Group discussion: How does money play an important role in the lives of individuals and their life of the church? *(Use T-Chart to write responses.)*

10:35   Questions to be addressed:

- What are some of the reasons we are uncomfortable about talking about money?
- Why must we spend time and energy necessary to understand financial realities as they relate to the ministry of the church?
- How can we as Christians do business and ministry more effectively?

11:00   **Break...10 minutes**

11:10   **Lesson 2:** Preparing for Growth and Harvest: Managing Money

11:45   Discussion and Q/A

11:55   Closing Prayer

SBJC Monthly Saturday Training Agenda

Facilitator: Pastor Jerome Lee, Jr. M.Div.

Module:	Spiritual Disciplines
Session 6:	Biblical Stewardship: Preparing for Growth and Harvest *(Part 2)*
Audience	Church Wide
Time Frame:	Saturday @ 10a.m-12:00 noon
Guiding Scripture:	*"To everything there is a season and a time to every purpose under the heaven,"* *Ecclesiastes 3:1*
Resources Used:	*Celebration of Discipline by Richard Foster*

9:50   Devotionals

10:00   Greetings and Overview

Review of Objectives   *At the end of this session, the participant will:*

- Be able to know and understand what tithing is.
- Be able to understand the importance of tithing.
- Be able to identify and understand the relationship between tithing and spirituality.

10:15   **Lesson 1:** Preparing for Growth and Harvest: Tithes & Offerings

Activity: Group discussion: What does God's word say about tithing? Look up scriptures.

10:35   Questions to be addressed:

- What is tithing?
- Why is tithing important?
- What is the relationship between tithing and spirituality?

11:00   **Break…………………………………………………………..10 minutes**

11:10   **Lesson 2:** Preparing for Growth and Harvest: Tithing and Spirituality

11:45   Discussion and Q/A

11:55   Closing Prayer

SBJC Monthly Saturday Training Agenda

Facilitator: Pastor Jerome Lee, Jr. M.Div.

Module:	Spiritual Disciplines
Session 7:	Biblical Stewardship: Preparing for Growth and Harvest *(Part 3)*
Audience:	Church Wide
Time Frame:	Saturday @ 10a.m-12:00 noon
Guiding Scripture:	*"To everything there is a season and a time to every purpose under the heaven," Ecclesiastes 3:1*
Resources Used:	*Celebration of Discipline by Richard Foster*

9:50   Devotionals

10:00   Greetings and Overview

Review of Objectives *At the end of this session, the participant will:*

- Be able to identify the three principles of giving.
- Be able to recognize and understand the importance of mission and giving.
- Discover ways in which God is helping you and your congregation to be a people of faith.

10:15   **Lesson 1**: Preparing for Growth and Harvest: Mission and Giving

Activity: Group discussion: What inspires you to give*? (List responses on chart paper).*

10:35   Questions to be addressed:

- What are the three principles of giving?

- How does giving make a difference in the lives of others?

- What is the relationship between mission and money?

11:00   **Break...10 minutes**

11:10   **Lesson 2:** Preparing for Growth and Harvest: A Winning Cause/A Spirit of Generosity

11:45   Discussion and Q/A

11:55   Closing Prayer

SBJC Monthly Saturday Training Agenda

Facilitator: Pastor Jerome Lee, Jr. M.Div.

Module:	Spiritual Disciplines
Session :	Biblical Stewardship: Preparing for Growth and Harvest *(Part 4)*
Audience:	Church wide
Time Frame:	Saturday @ 10a.m-12:00 noon
Guiding Scriptur	*"To everything there is a season and a time to every purpose under the heaven,"* *Ecclesiastes 3:1*
Resources Used	*Celebration of Discipline by Richard Foster*

9:50   Devotionals

10:00   Greetings and Overview

Review of Objectives   *At the end of this session, the participant will:*

- Be able to identify the six sources of giving.
- Understand the relative value of money.
- Understand that money is simply an effective, helpful means to advance God's mission.

10:15 **Lesson 1:** Preparing for Growth and Harvest: Six Sources of Giving

Activity: Discussion question: What are some reasons people don't give?
(Answers can be written on sticky note and placed on chart paper for discussion.)

10:35 Questions to be addressed:

- What are the six sources of giving?
- Why are these six sources of giving Important?
- How can all the giving possibilities be developed with your congregation?

11:00 **Break...10 minutes**

11:10 **Lesson 2:** Preparing for Growth and Harvest: Money for Mission

11:45 Discussion and Q/A

11:55 Closing Prayer

SJBC Weekly Bible Study Agenda

Facilitator: Pastor Jerome Lee, Jr. M.Div.

Module:	Spiritual Disciplines
Session 9:	What is Worship?
Audience:	Bible Study participants
Time Frame:	Tuesday @ 7pm and Wednesday @12 noon
Guiding Scripture:	*"O worship the Lord in the beauty of holiness: fear before him, all the earth"* *Psalm 96:9*
Resources Used:	*Delesslyn A. Kennebrew http://www.christianitytoday.com/biblestudies/bible-answers/spirituallllife/what-is-true-worship.html*

6:45   Devotionals

7:00   Greetings and Review of Objectives (*At the end of this unit, the participant will be able to*)

> Understand what true worship is……
> - The **Purpose** of worship
> - The **Priority** of worship
> - The **Person** we worship
> - The **Promise** of worship

7:10   **Activity:** On a 3x5 card, ask the participants to write their own personal definition of worship. (2 minutes); Turn and talk to a neighbor and share their definition of worship. Then share out with everyone.

7:30   **Lecture** on the purpose, priority, person and promise of worship

> (Approximately 15 minutes on each)

8:30   **Activity:** On the back of their 3x5 card, write what their definition of worship is since the training.

8:45   Closing Prayer

SJBC Weekly Bible Study Agenda

Facilitator: Pastor Jerome Lee, Jr. M.Div.

Module:	Spiritual Disciplines
Session 10:	What is Worship: An Old Testament Look
Audience:	Bible Study participants
Time Frame:	Tuesday @ 7pm and Wednesday @12 noon
Guiding Scripture:	*"O worship the Lord in the beauty of holiness: fear before him, all the earth"* *Psalm 96:9*
Resources Used:	Delesslyn A. Kennebrew *http://www.christianitytoday.com/biblestudies/bible-answers/spiritualllife/what-is-true-worship.html*; *http://www.gobible.org/bible/5.php*

6:45   Devotionals

7:00   Greetings and Review of Objectives (*At the end of this unit, the participant will):*

- Review the purpose, priority, person, and the promise of worship
- Understand how worship is viewed in the Old Testament

7:10   **Activity:** In groups of 4, ask each group member to review the purpose, priority, person and promise of worship.

7:30   **Lecture:**

- Worship in Genesis: Two Classes of Worshippers (Genesis 4 & 22)
- Worship in Exodus: Understand Who God Is (Ex. 3, 20, & 32; 1 Chronicles 15, and 2 Samuel 6)
- The Sabbath and Worship (Genesis 1-2, Exodus 20, Colossians 1)
- Worship and Song and Praise (Psalms 32 & 51, 2 Samuel 22)
- Worship in the Psalms (Psalms 19, 49, & 73)

8:30   Discussion Q/A

8:45   Closing Prayer

APPENDIX M 4

Module 4: Basic Ministry Skills

Session 1:   Growing Through Church Hurt: *Steps in Understanding Church Hurt*

Session 2:   Growing Through Church Hurt: *Dealing with Church Hurt God's Way*

Session 3:   Growing Through Church Hurt: *7 Ways to Heal After Church Conflict*

Session 4:   Protecting Church Unity: *A Biblical Background*

Session 5:   Protecting Church Unity: *Preventing Disunity*

Session 6:   Protecting Church Unity: *Breaking the Cycle*

Session 7:   Visitation in the Home or Hospital *(Part 1)*

Session 8:   Visitation in the Home or Hospital *(Part 2)*

Session 9:   Five Practices of Fruitful Congregations: *Overview*

Session 10:   Five Practices of Fruitful Congregations: *Radical Hospitality*

Session 11:   Five Practices of Fruitful Congregations: *Passionate Worship (Lesson 1)*

Session 12:   Five Practices of Fruitful Congregations: *Passionate Worship (Lesson 2 & 3)*

Session 13:   Five Practices of Fruitful Congregations: *Passionate Worship (Lesson 4 &5)*

Session 14:   Five Practices of Fruitful Congregations: *Intentional Faith Development*

Session 15:   Five Practices of Fruitful Congregations: *Risk-Taking Mission and Service*

Session 16:   Five Practices of Fruitful Congregations: *Extravagant Generosity*

SBJC Monthly Saturday Training Agenda

Facilitator: Pastor Jerome Lee, Jr. M.Div.

Module:	Basic Ministry Skills
Session 1:	Growing Through Church Hurt: Steps in Understanding Church Hurt
Audience:	Deacons and Deaconesses
Time Frame:	10:00-12:00 noon
Guiding Scripture:	*"(love) does not behave rudely, does not seek its own, is not provoked, thinks no evil." 1 Cor. 13*
Resources Used:	*http://powertochange.com/experience/spiritual-growth/hurtingchurch/*

9:50   Devotionals

10:00   Greetings and Overview

Review of Objectives   *At the end of this session, the participant will:*

- Be able to identify what church hurt is and its causes
- Be able to identify 5 key steps in addressing church hurt
- Be able to apply relevant scripture to address church hurt

10:15   **Lesson 1**: Growing Through Church Hurt: Background

Activity: What does Church Hurt: look like, sound like, feel like 10 mins.

10:35   Lecture: Questions to be addressed:

- What is Church Hurt?
- Why is it important to address?
- How does it impact your relationship with other church members?

11:00   **Break...10 minutes**

11:10   **Lesson 2:** Growing Through Church Hurt: Steps for addressing Church   Hurt:

- Step 1: Know Your Enemy   *1 Peter 5:8, Ephesians 6:11*
- Step 2: Keep Short Accounts   *Hebrews 12:15, Matthew 12:34*
- Step 3: Be Accountable   *Psalm 15, Proverbs 3:5,6*
- Step 4: Acknowledge Pride   *James 4:6, Romans 12:18*
- Step 5: Turn the Page   *James 3: 13-17*

11:45   Discussion and Q/A

11:55   Closing Prayer

SBJC Monthly Saturday Training Agenda

Facilitator: Pastor Jerome Lee, Jr. M.Div.

Module:	Basic Ministry Skills
Session 2:	Growing Through Church Hurt: Dealing with Church Hurt God's Way
Audience:	Deacons and Deaconesses
Time Frame:	10:00-12:00 noon
Guiding Scripture:	*"(love) does not behave rudely, does not seek its own, is not provoked, thinks no evil." 1 Cor. 13*
Resources Used:	*http://www.charismamag.com/blogs/the-plumb-line/19592-dealing-with-church-hur-gods*

9:50	Devotionals
10:00	Greetings and Overview
	Review of Objectives *At the end of this session, the participant will:*
	• Be able to identify appropriate means to address Church Hurt • Be able to understand that Forgiveness is a means to confront Church Hurt
10:15	**Review:** Session 1: 5 Steps in Understanding Church Hurt *(The Facilitator will ask the participants what the steps are and what do they mean)*
10:30	**Lesson 3**: 4 Ways to Deal with Church Hurt God's Way (Part 1)
	• Take it to God: Pray Psalms 50:15 • Don't Retaliate Matt. 5:38, 44
11:00	**Break...10 minutes**
11:10	**Lesson 3:** 4 Ways to Deal with Church Hurt God's Way (Part 2)
	• Let the Lord Work 1 Peter 4:8 • Learn to Forgive Matt. 6:14
11:40	**Activity:** Give each participant a sheet of notebook paper. Have the participant to think of someone who has hurt them in the church. Then have them to write a letter to someone that they need to forgive.
11:50	Discussion and Q/A
12:00	Closing Prayer

SBJC Monthly Saturday Training Agenda

Facilitator: Pastor Jerome Lee, Jr. M.Div.

Module:	Basic Ministry Skills
Session 3:	Growing Through Church Hurt: 7 Ways to Heal After Church Conflict
Audience:	Deacons and Deaconesses
Time Frame:	Tuesday @ 7pm and Wednesday @12 noon
Guiding Scripture:	*"(love) does not behave rudely, does not seek its own, is not provoked, thinks no evil." 1 Cor. 13*
Resources Used:	*http://www.pbs.org/thecongregation/indepth/sevenways.html*

6:45   Devotionals

7:00   Greetings and Review of Objectives (*At the end of this session, the participant will be able to):*

- Define Church Conflict
- Identify 7 ways to heal after a church conflict

7:10   **Activity:** Pose the question to the audience: "Why does the words church fight seem oxymoronic?" Have participants to **turn and talk** with neighbor and then have some responses shared out with everyone.

7:20   **Activity:** On chart paper, solicit responses from the audience of ways they believe one can heal from church fight.

7:30   **Lecture and Discussion:**

1. Pray
2. Stay purposefully connected
3. Be honest
4. Listen for feelings
5. Allow for differences
6. Find the lessons
7. Prepare for next time

8:30   **Activity:** Have participants to break into groups of 3 praying for congregation and each other with regard to being hurt in the church.

8:50   Closing Prayer

SJBC Deacon/Deaconess Training Agenda

Facilitator: Pastor Jerome Lee, Jr. M.Div.

Module:	*Basic Ministry Skills*
Session 4:	*Protecting Church Unity: Biblical Principals of Unity*
Audience:	*Deacons and Deaconesses*
Time Frame:	*Saturday @ 10a.m-12:00 noon and **2nd & 4th Thursday @ 6:30-8:30 pm***
Guiding Scripture:	*"Being diligent to preserve the unity of the Spirit in the bond of peace..." Ephesians 4:3-6*
Resources Used:	*The Baptist Deacon by Robert Naylor ; http://www.thestraitgate.org/devotionals/faith-at-work-/protecting-the-unity-of-the-church;*

6:15   Devotionals

6:30   Greetings and Review of Objectives: participants will be able to
- understand the biblical principal of Church Unity
- discuss elements necessary to continue in Unity
- understand the role of the Deacon/Pastor in maintaining Unity

6:35   **Activity:** Participants write their own personal definition of unity. (*Have participants to share with the persons beside them and create 1definition together. Write their partner definition on a piece of construction paper. Post definitions around the room). Have a representative to read the definition of unity.)*

7:00   Lecture: Understanding the Scriptures:

- Ephesians 4:3-6
- Romans 12:4-5
- John 17:21

8:00   Question posed to the group: If Jesus prayed for unity and called us to protect it, how do we do that? (Allow for responses for approximately 5 minutes).

8:05   We Protect Unity By:

- Be aware of the power of our words
- Practice the art of forgiveness
- Regularly get into the Word of God

8:30   **Activity:** Break participants up into groups of 4 to pray for specific areas of the church:(i.e. Pastor, Deacon/Deaconess Ministry, Children's Department, Senior, Young Adult Ministries, Finances, Outreach, etc.)

8:45   Closing Prayer

SJBC Deacon/Deaconess Training Agenda

Facilitator: Pastor Jerome Lee, Jr. M.Div.

Module:	Basic Ministry Skills
Session 5:	Protecting Church Unity: *Preventing Disunity*
Audience:	Deacons and Deaconesses
Time Frame:	Saturday @ 10a.m-12:00 noon and **2nd & 4th Thursday @ 6:30-8:30 pm**
Guiding Scripture:	*"Being diligent to preserve the unity of the Spirit in the bond of peace"* *Ephesians 4:3-6*
Resources Used:	*The Baptist Deacon by Robert Naylor;* *http://www.baptiststart.com/deacon.htm#path*

6:15   Devotionals

6:30   Greetings and Review of Objectives   *Participants will:*

- Be able to identify ways to prevent disunity
- Be able to Identify the causes of disunity
- Be able to understand their role in maintaining Unity

6:35   **Activity:** Have participants to turn and talk and discuss the meaning of the following quote from Robert Naylor's book: The Baptist Deacon on pg. 11.

"When a man becomes a deacon, he loses the privilege, if such exists, of participating in a church ro. A member of the ranks may claim that often-abused privilege, 'speaking his mind.' When a man becomes a deacon-selected and called by the Holy Spirit, chosen by the church, dedicated by personal choice-he forfeits the right to promote in any fashion, a division in the life of the church. The one inescapable duty of the deacon in the New Testament was the protection of the church fellowship."

7:00   **Pose the question:** What causes disunity? Participants will share before giving the reasons for disunity.

- Disunity is caused by:_____, _____,_____, _____
- Preventing Disunity by:
  o Early Detection System
  o Apprehend, Foresee, and Take Steps to Avoid Danger
  o Don't let Sleeping Dogs Lie

8:00   How can the Deacon and Pastor work together to combat disunity?

8:30   **Activity:** Summarizing activity called 3-2-1: (List 3 ways to cause disunity; 2-ways to prevent disunity and 1-way the deacon and the pastor can work together for unity.

8:45   Closing Prayer

SJBC Deacon/Deaconess Agenda

Facilitator: Pastor Jerome Lee, Jr. M.Div.

Module:	Basic Ministry Skills
Session 6:	Protecting Church Unity: *Breaking the Cycle*
Audience:	Deacons and Deaconesses
Time Frame: **pm**	Saturday @ 10a.m-12:00 noon and **2nd & 4th Thursday @ 6:30-8:30**
Guiding Scripture:	*"Being diligent to preserve the unity of the Spirit in the bond of peace…"* *Ephesians 4:3-6*
Resources Used:	*http://powertochange.com/experience/spiritual-growth/hurtingchurch/* *http://www.baptiststart.com/deacon.htm#path*

6:15   Devotionals

6:30   Greetings and Review of Objectives   *At the end of this session, the participant*
will:

- Be able to understand that the hurting church is not an occasional dilemma
- Be able to identify steps in breaking the cycle of church hurt
- Be able to recognize that each step is based in love

6:40   **Activity:** In small groups, brainstorm: What are some steps we can create to make dealing with church hurt proactive rather than reactive? Have groups to put information on charts and post around the room. Then groups report out.

7:00   **Lecture and Discussion:** *(Solicit volunteers to read each scripture)*

1. Know your enemy (Ephesians 6:12; 1 Peter 5:8, 9; John 10:10)
2. Keep short accounts (Hebrews 12:15; Matthew 12:34; Proverbs 4:23)
3. Don't be afraid of accountability (Proverbs 3:5, 6; Titus 3:10)
4. Acknowledge pride (James 4:6; Romans 12:18; 1 Corinthians 13)
5. Be willing to plant stakes in the ground (James 3:13-17)

8:15   **Write** the scripture on the board: *"By this all men will know that you are my disciples, if you love one another." (John 13:35)* and **discuss** ways that love can help us with the fulfillment of right living that God calls us to do. Ask participants to give other scriptures on love to support the process.

8:45   Closing Prayer

SBJC Monthly Saturday Training Agenda

Facilitator: Pastor Jerome Lee, Jr. M.Div.

Module:	Basic Ministry Skills
Session 7:	Visitation in the Home or Hospital (Part 1)
Audience:	Deacons and Deaconesses
Time Frame:	10:00-12:00 noon
Guiding Scripture:	*"Is any sick among you? Let him call for the elders of the church…;"* *James 5:14-15*
Resources Used:	www.lcgi.org/church-health-growth/visitation-ministry-training

9:50   Devotionals

10:00   Greetings and Overview

Review of Objectives   *At the end of this session, the participant will:*

- Be able to understand the biblical perspective on visiting
- Be able to understand why visiting is important
- Be able to discuss relevant considerations when visiting

10:15   **Lesson 1**: Introduction- Visitation in the Home or Hospital

Exercise: Solicit 6 members to participate in a skit showing the wrong way to visit someone that is sick in the hospital

10:25   Have participants to share aloud the wrongs that were shown (Write on chart paper)

10:35   Lecture: What does the Bible say about visiting the sick? How do you prepare yourself spiritually and emotionally for the visit?

11:00   **Break………………………………………10 minutes**

11:10   **Lesson 2:** Facilitator: Deacon Hobson Bryant, PAC.

Lecture:

- Understanding the hospital patient's world
- Explanations of patients'' possible emotional, financial, family, and spiritual distress
- Do's and Don'ts to note before and during a visit to the patient's room

11:45   **Exercise:** The facilitator will solicit 6 different participants to redo the skit from the beginning of the lesson. Then share aloud the differences between the 2 skits.

12:00   Closing Prayer

SJBC Monthly Saturday Training Agenda

Facilitator: Pastor Jerome Lee, Jr. M.Div.

Module:	Basic Ministry Skills
Session 8:	Visitation in the Home or Hospital (Part 2)
Audience:	Deacons and Deaconesses
Time Frame:	10:00-12:00 noon
Guiding Scripture	*"I was sick, and you visited me..." Matthew 25:36*
Resources Used:	www.lcgi.org/church-health-growth/visitation-ministry-training

9:50	Devotionals
10:00	Greetings and Overview
	Review of Objectives *(At the end of this session, the participant will be able to:*

- Discuss relevant considerations when visiting
  - Shut Ins
  - Difficult patients
  - Dying
  - Alzheimer's or Comatose patients
- Discuss ways to pray for those on our Healing and Recovery List at SJBC

10:10	**Activity**: The participants will get in groups of 4 creating a poster of Do's or Don'ts for Visitation in the Hospital (*Materials: Markers, construction paper);* After which the participants will present their posters as a review of the materials.
10:30	Discussion:

- Special Needs of Shut-ins
- Ministering to difficult patients

11:00	**Break...10 minutes**
11:10	Discussion:

- Ministering to the Dying
- Ministering to Alzheimer's or Comatose patients

11:35	**Activity:** Role Play *(Solicit for volunteers to role play visiting a member in Hospice.)*
11:45	How should we pray for those on our Healing and Recovery list?
12:00	Closing Prayer

SJBC Weekly Bible Study Agenda

Facilitator: Pastor Jerome Lee, Jr. M.Div.

Module:	Basic Ministry Skills
Session 9:	Five Practices of Fruitful Congregations: Overview
Audience:	Bible Study participants
Time Frame:	Tuesday @ 7pm and Wednesday @12 noon
Guiding Scripture:	*"I was a stranger and you welcomed me" Matthew 25:35*
Resources Used:	*Five Practices of Fruitful Congregations by Robert Schnase*

6:45   Devotionals

7:00   Greetings and Review of Objectives *(At the end of this session, the participant will be able to)*

- Understand the 5 Practices of a Fruitful Congregation
- Assess current practices at SJBC
- Prioritize current practices at SJBC
- Identify areas of growth within the church

7:15   **Pre-Assessment** of Current Practices at SJBC *(Give everyone a 3x5 card and label it A-E; Explain to the audience that they will rate each statement 1-5, with 5 being the highest. Read aloud a list of 5 statements to rate. After completion, ask the participants to rate these items from with regards to importance from 1-5, with 1 being most important.)* APPENDEX I

7:35   Discuss assessment orally about their ratings

7:50   Introduce the book: <u>5 Practices of Fruitful Congregation</u> and present an overview of the 5 Practices *(Approximately 10 minutes each)*

- Practice 1: The Practice of Radical Hospitality
- Practice 2: The Practice of Passionate Worship
- Practice 3: The Practice of Intentional Faith Development
- Practice 4: The Practice of Risk-Taking Mission and Service
- Practice 5: The Practice of Extravagant Generosity

8:30   **Activity:** Talking Point: "These fundamental practices are so critical to a congregation's mission that failure to perform them in an exemplary way results in congregational deterioration and decline. *(Have participants to talk in small groups sharing their understanding of the statement.)*

8:45   Discuss with whole group

8:50   Closing Prayer

SJBC Weekly Bible Study Agenda

Facilitator: Pastor Jerome Lee, Jr. M.Div.

Module:	Basic Ministry Skills
Session 10:	Five Practices of Fruitful Congregations: Radical Hospitality
Audience:	Bible Study participants
Time Frame:	Tuesday @ 7pm and Wednesday @12 noon
Guiding Scripture:	*"Welcome one another, therefore, just as Christ has welcomed you, for the glory of God." (Romans 15:7).*
Resources Used:	*Five Practices of Fruitful Congregations by Robert Schnase*

6:45   Devotionals

7:00   Greetings and Review of Objectives (*At the end of this session, the participant will be able to:*

- Define Radical Hospitality
- What does Radical Hospitality look like at SJBC?
- Identify areas of growth within the church

7:10   **Activity:** Pose the question to the audience: "What is hospitality?" Have participants to **turn and talk** with neighbor and then have some responses shared out with everyone.

7:20   Lessons 1: The Practice of Radical Hospitality

8: 10   **Activity:** Turn and Talk to discuss the statement and question: How does the physical structure and the people at SJBC make you feel welcomed. Question: What does hospitality look like at SJBC?

8:30   Share out discussions about the statement

8:45   Summarize lesson on Radical Hospital

8:50   Closing Prayer

SJBC Monthly Saturday Training Agenda

Facilitator: Pastor Jerome Lee, Jr. M.Div.

Module:	Basic Ministry Skills
Session 11:	Five Practices of Fruitful Congregations: Passionate Worship- (Lesson 1)
Audience:	Bible Study participants
Time Frame:	Tuesday @ 7pm and Wednesday @12 noon
Guiding Scripture:	*"Welcome one another, therefore, just as Christ has welcomed you, for the glory of God." (Romans 15:7).*
Resources Used:	*Five Practices of Fruitful Congregations by Robert Schnase*

6:45   Devotionals

7:00   Greetings and Review of Objectives (*At the end of this session, the participant will be able to):*

- Review what is Radical Hospitality
- Define Worship
- Define Passionate Worship
- Preparing for Worship

7:10   Review: What is Radical Hospitality? (Pose the questions to participants to answer aloud.).

7:20   **Activity:** Give everyone a 3x5 card. On one side, write their definition of *worship* and on the other side write their definition of *praise*. Collect cards.

7:35   Read a few of the responses and discuss (Have a volunteer to write common themes from the comments on a piece of large chart paper).

7:50   Discussion: Passionate Worship

8:30   **Activity**: Tell your neighbor how you prepare for worship service. Share out.

8:40   Summarize lesson

8:55   Closing Prayer

SJBC Weekly Bible Study Agenda

Facilitator: Pastor Jerome Lee, Jr. M.Div.

Module:	Basic Ministry Skills
Session 12:	Five Practices of Fruitful Congregations: Passionate Worship-(Lessons: 2& 3)
Audience:	Bible Study participants
Time Frame:	Tuesday @ 7pm and Wednesday @12 noon
Guiding Scripture:	*"Welcome one another, therefore, just as Christ has welcomed you, for the glory of God." (Romans 15:7).*
Resources Used:	*Five Practices of Fruitful Congregations by Robert Schnase*

6:45   Devotionals

7:00   Greetings and Review of Objectives

- Review Passionate Worship
- Verbalize what Passionate Worship is NOT
- Analyze their worship experience

7:10   **Activity:** Divide participants into 3 big groups by counting off in 3s. Once the groups are divided, assign one of the questions listed below for them to discuss.

1. Think about this past Sunday's service. In what specific ways was passionate worship displayed?
1. What evidence did a guest or newcomers observe that demonstrated passionate worship?
2. What evidence of radical hospitality or any hospitality demonstrated?

7:50   Each group select two representatives to discuss their questions with the class.

8:10   Questions and Answers

8:30   Summarize lesson on worship

8:45   Closing Prayer

SJBC Weekly Bible Study Agenda

Facilitator: Pastor Jerome Lee, Jr. M.Div.

Module:	Basic Ministry Skills
Session 13:	Five Practices of Fruitful Congregations: Passionate Worship-(Lessons: 4 & 5)
Audience:	Bible Study participants
Time Frame:	Tuesday @ 7pm and Wednesday @12 noon
Guiding Scripture	*"Welcome one another, therefore, just as Christ has welcomed you, for the glory of God." (Romans 15:7).*
Resources Used:	*Five Practices of Fruitful Congregations by Robert Schnase*

6:45   Devotionals

7:00   Greetings and Review of Objectives (*At the end of this session, the participant will):*

- Describe their own *passionate worship* style
- Identify the pre-dominant worship style of SJBC
- Describe passionate worship changes lives

7:10   Review last week's lesson and Discuss:

- What difference does the practice of *passionate worship* make?
- What evidence do you have of that difference?
- What role does the Pastor play in passionate worship?

7:40   **Activity:** Have participants to turn and talk to their neighbors. Write the differences on 3x5 cards:

What is the difference if any in the worship experience between regular Sunday Service, Easter, Christmas, and Mother's Day?

7:50   Lesson 5:

- What are the Roles in Worship?
- Preparation for Worship?

8:30   Questions and Answers

8:40   Summarize lesson

8:50   Closing Prayer

SJBC Weekly Bible Study Agenda

Facilitator: Pastor Jerome Lee, Jr. M.Div.

Module:	Basic Ministry Skills
Session 14:	Five Practices of Fruitful Congregations: Intentional Faith Development
Audience:	Bible Study participants
Time Frame:	Tuesday @ 7pm and Wednesday @12 noon
Guiding Scripture	*"They devoted themselves to the apostles' teaching and fellowship, to the breaking of bread and the prayers." (Acts 2:42).*
Resources Used:	*Five Practices of Fruitful Congregations by Robert Schnase*

6:45   Devotionals

7:00   Greetings and Review of Objectives (*At the end of this session, the participant will):*

- Define Intentional Faith Development
- Describe how disciples are best formed
- List and describes the Fruit of the spirit
- Explain the importance of bible study

7:10   Introduction to Intentional Faith Development

- What is Intentional Faith Development?
- How does one grow in Christ?
- How is your faith intentional and purposeful?

7:45   **Activity:** Turn and Talk: Discuss a time when you had to utilize intentional and purposeful faith?

7:55   Share out after 10 minute discussion.

8:25   Questions and Answers

8:35   Summarize lesson

8:45   Closing Prayer

SJBC Weekly Bible Study Agenda

Facilitator: Pastor Jerome Lee, Jr. M.Div.

Module:	Basic Ministry Skills
Session 15:	Five Practices of Fruitful Congregations: The Practice of Risk-Taking Mission & Service
Audience:	Bible Study participants
Time Frame:	Tuesday @ 7pm and Wednesday @12 noon
Guiding Scripture	*Truly I tell you, just as you did it to one of the least of these who are members of my family, you did it to me." Matthew 25:40*
Resources Used:	*Five Practices of Fruitful Congregations by Robert Schnase*

6:45   Devotionals

7:00   Greetings and Review of Objectives *(At the end of this session, the participant will):*

- Define Risk-taking mission and Service
- Describe what Risk-taking mission and service looks like
- Understand the opportunities for mission in the Greensboro community.

7:10   Review of previous lesson

Lecture: (Questions to be discussed)

- What are missions and its impact?
- How do missions impact the local community?
- How is missions considered the church's life blood?

7:40   **Activity**: On a 3x5 card, have the participants to place one question on each side;

- What concerns you have about missions?
- Why won't you go (i.e. In our community, the city of Greensboro, N.C. etc.)?

8:00   **Activity**: In groups of 6, have participants to search the Scriptures: (How does the scripture relate to Risk-taking mission & service? Use the scriptures to make real world applications to further explain its relevance.

- Psalms 99:4
- Psalms 33:
- Luke 4:18-1
- Psalms 82:3

- Micah 6:8
- Matthew 25:35-37
- Matthew 20:26-28

8:50   Closing Prayer

SJBC Weekly Bible Study Agenda

Facilitator: Pastor Jerome Lee, Jr. M.Div.

Module:	Basic Ministry Skills
Session 16: Generosity	Five Practices of Fruitful Congregations: The Practice of Extravagant
Audience:	Bible Study participants
Time Frame:	Tuesday @ 7pm and Wednesday @12 noon
Guiding Scripture	*"You will be enriched in every way for your great generosity." 2 Corinthians 9:11*
Resources Used:	*Five Practices of Fruitful Congregations by Robert Schnase*

6:45   Devotionals

7:00   Greetings and Review of Objectives *(At the end of this session, the participant will)*:

- Be able to define Tithing and Generosity
- Be able to discuss the biblical background for tithing

7:10   **Activity**: Divide participants into 3 large sections and assign a question to each. Pose the questions: What does generosity mean? What does generosity look like in church? Why does Paul consider generosity as one of the "Fruit of the spirit"? (See Galatians 5:22).

7:20   Share out responses to questions and discuss.

7:30   Introduce Tithing using a KWL chart. Ask participants to write everything that they know about tithing and what would they like to know. Have a large piece of chart paper and write down the responses of the participants for what they already know and what they want to know.

7:45   Tithing and giving in the Old Testament

- Genesis 14:20   Amos 5:21-24
- Exodus 35:5   Malachi 3:8-10

8:15   Giving in the New Testament:

Luke 21:1-4   Luke 10:35   Luke 12:13-21

8:40   **Activity:** Define what extravagant generosity is (KWL)

8:55   Closing Prayer

APPENDIX M5:

Module 5: Deacon Partnership With The Pastor

Session 1:   Effective Deacon Pastor Relationships

Session 2:   Seven Ways to Hurt Your Pastor

Session 3:   The Power of the Tongue

Session 4:   Deacon/Pastor Partnership

Session 5:   Servant Leadership

SJBC Deacon/Deaconess Training Agenda

Facilitator: Pastor Jerome Lee, Jr. M.Div.

Module:	Deacon Partnership with the Pastor
Session 1:	Effective Deacon Pastor Relationships
Audience:	Deacons and Deaconesses
Time Frame:	Saturday @ 10a.m-12:00 noon and 2nd & 4th Thursday @ 6:30-8:30 pm
Guiding Scripture:	Acts 6:1 and Quote: *"There is not a greater blessing in a pastor's life than a Godly deacon who loves the Lord and loves the Word of God."*----Derek Gentle
Resources Used:	*http://www.baptiststart.com/pastors_deacon.htm*

6:20   Devotionals

6:40   Greetings and Overview

Review of Objective At the end of this session, the participants will:

- Explore aspects of a good pastor/deacon relationship
- Understand the need for strong encouragement from deacons
- Analyze the need for Pastor's spiritual health barometer

6:50   **Lesson 1:** Effective Pastor-Deacon Relationships

Activity: Turn and talk to your neighbor: "Is the relationship with your pastor a relationship you trust" Discuss with the group.

7:05   Lecture: Questions to be addressed:

- Does the office of Pastor and the deacons appreciate each other enough?
- Understanding the level of stress Pastors live with?
- Understanding each other's spiritual gifts.

7:50   **Lesson 2:** Pastor's spiritual health barometer (Discussion)

- Deacon/deaconess transferring church membership
- Who is looking out for the pastor?
- The church is not a business. The church is on a mission to win souls for Christ.

8:25   Closing Prayer

SBJC Monthly Saturday Training Agenda

Facilitator: Pastor Jerome Lee, Jr. M.Div.

Module:	Deacon Partnership with the Pastor
Session 2:	Seven Ways to Hurt your Pastor
Audience:	Deacons and Deaconesses
Time Frame:	**Saturday @ 10am-12:00 noon** and Thursday @ 6:30 pm
Guiding Scripture:	*"If anyone considers himself religious and yet does not keep a tight rein on his tongue, he deceives himself and his religion is worthless."*
Resources Used:	http://thomrainer.com/2014/06/16/seven-ways-hurt-pastor/

9:45   Devotionals

10:00   Greetings and Review of Objectives s *(At the end of this session, the participant will):*

- What does the Bible say about the tongue?
- Understand how the tongue is used to hurt the pastor

10:10   **Activity:** Opening Questions: If you were assigned by the devil to hurt the pastor, what would you do or say? *(On a 3x5 card, write your responses and then share out)*

10:25   Lesson 1: Taming of the Tongue": Part 1-A Look at the book of James tells us about our unruly tongues and teaches us the difference between man's wisdom and God's wisdom.

11:00   **Break...10 minutes**

11:10   Lesson 2: 7 Ways to Hurt Your Pastor

1. Criticize the Pastor's family
2. Tell the Pastor he is overpaid
3. Don't defend the Pastor
4. Tell your pastor what an easy job he has
5. Be a constant naysayer
6. Make comments about the pastor's expenditures
7. Compare your pastor's preaching and ministry unfavorably to that of another pastor

11:40   **Activity:** In groups of 4, draw a web on chart paper and write ways to encourage your pastor then share out

11:50   Closing Prayer

SJBC Deacon/Deaconess Training Agenda

Facilitator: Pastor Jerome Lee, Jr. M.Div.

Module:	Deacon Partnership with the Pastor
Session 3:	The Power of the Tongue
Audience:	Deacons and Deaconess
Time Frame:	Saturday @ 10am-12:00 noon and **Thursday @ 6:30-8:30 pm**
Guiding Scripture:	*"Wherefore he saith, When he ascended up on high, he led captivity captive, and gave gifts unto men," Ephesians 4:8*
Resources Used:	*http://ministry-to-children.com/tongue-lesson/* ; *https://bible.org/seriespage/lesson-12-taming-terrible-tongue-james-31-12*

6:15   Devotionals

6:30   Greetings and Review of Objectives s *(At the end of this session, the participant will):*

- What does the Bible say about the tongue?
- Examine 4 Truths in taming the tongue

6:40   **Activity: Questions for Group Discussion**
Do you find that you are more likely to be critical, gossip or use harsh language with some of your friends than others? If so, why ?
     • Why do you think James says no [human] can tame the tongue?
     • What are some ways to steer a gossip fest or trash-talk session in another direction? Why might it be important to do so?
     • Have you ever had something you've said about someone else come back to haunt you? Describe the situation.

7:00   **Activity:** *Break the participants into two big groups.* Read James 3:1-12 aloud. Assign the first group the task of listening for the ways that James compares the tongue. Assign the second group the task of listening for the importance of controlling the things that they say. Share out.

7:30   **Lecture:** Examine 4 Truths in Taming the Tongue. (Q &A following)
1. To tame the tongue, we must recognize that we will be held accountable for what we say (3:1-2).
2. To tame the tongue, we must recognize its power for good or for evil (3:3-5a).
3. To tame the tongue, we must recognize that it is a humanly untamable source of terrible evil (3:5b-8).
4. To tame the tongue, we must recognize that its inconsistencies are rooted in its source (3:9-12).

8:30   Closing Prayer

SJBC Deacon/Deaconess Training Agenda

Facilitator: Pastor Jerome Lee, Jr. M.Div.

Module:	Deacon Partnership with the Pastor
Session 4:	Deacon/Pastor Partnership
Audience:	Deacons and Deaconess
Time Frame:	Saturday @ 10am-12:00 noon and **Thursday @ 6:30-8:30 pm**
Guiding Scripture:	*"Wherefore he saith, When he ascended up on high, he led captivity captive, and gave gifts unto men," Ephesians 4:8*
Resources Used:	*http://www.baptiststart.com/pastors_deacons.htm*; *http://www.lifeway.com/Article/chrch-ministry-healthy-deacon-pastor-relationships*; *http://www.lifeway.com/Article/chrch-ministry-effective-deacon-pastor-relationships*;

6:15   Devotionals

6:30   Greetings and Review of Objectives *(At the end of this session, the participant will)*:

- Review 3 articles about deacon/pastor partnership.
- Identify ways in which this partnership can be created.

6:40   **Activity:** Have participants to count off in 3's. Assign a specific article to each of the 3 groups. Have them to read and discuss. Then have each group create a chart summarizing the important points of the article.

- "Healthy Deacon-Pastor Relationships"
- "Effective Pastor-Deacon Relationship"
- "What Pastors Wish Deacons Knew"

7:30   Have representatives from each group present their chart which summarizes the article.

8:00   Discuss with participants what each article has in common; what are some other ways to facilitate a better relationship with the pastor.

8:25   Closing Prayer

SJBC Deacon/Deaconess Agenda

Facilitator: Pastor Jerome Lee, Jr. M.Div.

Module:	Deacon Partnership with the Pastor
Session 5:	Servant Leadership
Audience:	Deacons and Deaconesses
Time Frame:	Saturday @ 10a.m-12:00 noon and **2nd & 4th Thursday @ 6:30-8:30 pm**
Guiding Scripture:	*For even the Son of Man came not to be served but to serve, and to give his life as a ransom for many." Mark10:45*
Resources Used:	*http://www.openbible.info/topics/servant_leaders* *http://www.gotquestions.org/servant-leadersip.html* *https://seminary.fresno.edu/resources/a-closer-look-at-servant-leadership*

6:20   Devotionals

6:40   Greetings and Overview

Review of Objective At the end of this session, the participants will:

- Be able to define servant leadership according to scripture.
- Be able to understand how Jesus Christ demonstrated servant leadership *(John 13:12-17)*.
- Be able to understand what Servant Leaders are NOT!

6:45   Pose the question, "What is Servant-Leadership?" Have each participant to put their responses on a 3x5 card then place their responses on a chart.

6:55   **Lecture:** Examine John 13:12-17

7:30   Principles of Servant Leadership

- Character of Humility
- Character of Teachability
- Character of Serving Others

8:00   Other Characteristics of Servant Leadership

8:20   Questions and Answers

8:30   Closing Prayer

APPENDIX N: Sermons

1. **N 1:** Crying Over Spilled Milk

2. **N 2:** What the Word Will Do

3. **N 3:** Strength in the Journey

4. **N 4:** A Perfect Posture for Ministry

5. **N 5:** What Real Friends Do

APPENDIX N 1:   CRYING OVER SPILLED MILK – SERMON OUTLINE
1 SAMUEL 16:1-7 (V-1)

PROPOSITION:

The phrase "crying over spilled milk" is a term that denotes the time that one can waste mourning, complaining or whining over some incident that happened in our life, whether it was something that we had control over or not.

It is a clear statement of the minutes, hours, days, weeks, months and years that can go by in which we could have cleaned up the mess and damage that has occurred, while moving on to another attempt to get what God still has for us.

THESIS

Then Samuel left for Ramah, but Saul went up to his home in Gibeah of Saul. Until the day Samuel died, he did not go to see Saul again, though Samuel mourned for him. And the Lord was grieved that he had made Saul king over Israel. (**1 Samuel 15:34-35**).

Then there is an interesting line that takes place in chapter 16:1…God has to take the initiative to step in and says to Samuel, how long will you mourn for Saul, being that I have rejected him as king over Israel?

ANTITHESIS:

There are times in our life, even within the ministry of the Lords Church that we spend a considerable length of time crying over decisions that God has deemed necessary for his people.

WHY DO WE CRY OVER SPILLED MILK? AND HOW CAN WE MOVE ON?

SYNTHESIS:

POINT I – Your head and your heart has to be on one accord.

The question, how long will you mourn for Saul is an implication that Samuel's head and heart were not on the same page, in fact they were out of rhythm.

Your head and your heart has to be on one accord – he allowed his head to separate from his heart, long enough for his head to dictate to him how long that he will sit here and cry over something that was in the will of God to happen.

POINT II – Maximize your moment.

The milk that Samuel was crying over – was over something that was out of his control. God did not have a problem with him mourning. I don't want to paint this picture of God being insensitive…because after all, Jesus did say cast your cares upon me for I careth for you.

God has a problem with him mourning too long. Crying over spilled milk to long is a clear indication of your spiritual immaturity.

POINT III - God is not going to just feed you, but there are other sheep that are not yet of this fold.

The work of the kingdom is a progressive work that must continue on. Therefore, God has already chosen a leader for his people to lead them in such a time as this. This leader will be the one chosen to go after the lost sheep of Israel, the lost sheep of the community, the lost sheep of your families.

CONCLUSION:

Pick up your crying towel and put on your dancing shoes and get ready to join God where he is already working.

God is working all around you and around this church. He's working in you and through you. Take an assessment of what God is doing in your life…REHEARSE some of them. Now unto him that is able to do exceeding abundantly above all that we ask or think, according to the power that worketh in us…**Ephesians 3:20**

APPENDIX N 2: WHAT THE WORD WILL DO – SERMON OUTLINE

EZEKIEL 37:1

PROPOSITION:

It goes without saying, that necessity is the mother of invention. With that being said, this statement definitely has some validity to it when we look at what God has done in His creation of the world and humanity. God in his infinite wisdom created a world and gave man a purpose.

God has a plan and purpose for our lives. "For I know the plans for you declares the Lord. Plans not to harm you, plans to give you hope and a future. (Jeremiah 29:11 NIV).

It was never in the will of God that lives be chaotic and confused.

It was never in the will of God that his church would be divided into us and them.

It was never in the will of God that chemical dependencies would dominate our culture.

However, it is in the will of God that he brings order to disorder and to fulfill the plans and purposes of his people.

THESIS:

The book of Ezekiel chronicles the prophet's life and ministry. Beginning with his call as a prophet and commissioning as a "watchman for the people of Israel", Ezekiel immediately began to preach and demonstrate God's truth, as he predicted the approaching siege and destruction of Jerusalem. God was illustrating what he intended to do with the exiled Jews. Though their nation was "dead," God would raise it to lie again. Ezekiel was speaking of a spiritual resurrection, not a physical one.

ANTITHESIS:

Sometimes we can fall so far into spiritual bondage and transgression that it can appear that our church, family, and our communities have no hope. When we look around and see what's going on around us, we ask ourselves that same question that God asked Ezekiel. Can these bones live? Like the prophet we must admit that only God knows.

Relevant question – Is there any hope for our church?

SYNTHESIS:

Relevant question – what must be the posture of those of us who anticipate Gods next move for us as a people, who are in desperate need of Hope and a future.

POINT I – Take an assessment of your life.

Ezekiel was asked, can these bones live? These bones once had life in them. These bones were at one time somebody's brother, somebody's father or son. And now they are disconnected from the blessings of God. They will never again experience the joy of life.

POINT II – You have to be inspired. (Hear the word of the Lord).

Prophesy to them. How, then, can they call on the one they have not believed in. And how can they believe in the one of whom they have not heard? And how can they hear without someone preaching to them? And how can anyone preach unless they are sent? As it is written: "How beautiful are the feet of those who bring good news!" **(Romans 10:4, 15)**

POINT III - Power of fulfillment. (Vision first).

You must believe in the power of fulfillment. You have to first be a witness, you have to first believe it. After you have seen God work in your own life, then you ought to have a witness that he can bring fulfillment in somebody else's life.

CONCLUSION:

The bones came together and stood as a great army. God raised them up from being warriors to worshippers. They died fighting, and fighting is what killed them. God did not raise you up from the valley of dry bones to go back to being what you were (warriors). He raised you up to be worshippers. That's what the word will do.

APPENDIX N 3: STRENGTH FOR THE JOURNEY

HABAKKUK 3:17-19

Proposition:

The question of theodicy "Why do bad things happen to good people?" is a question that has pondered the minds of many people who have felt that their tragedy should not have happened to them. The truth is no one really expects to be overcome by injustice or deprivation, especially if we are Christians who profess to trust in God. Just because we are baptized believers in Jesus Christ, that does not exempt us from the evil of this world.

Thesis:

Who understood this more than the people of Judah, a southern group of people who had historically been torn away from their northern brothers and sisters Israel. Each nation has had their own dispute with ungodly nations whose will was to impose their god and culture on them. Different from most prophets who usually speak God's word to us, Habakkuk speaks our words to God. He articulates our pains, hurts, and disappointments but still celebrates despite the fact that the fig trees are not blossoming, no grapes on the vine, the crops failed to yield and no cattle in the stall. Still we have something to celebrate. The celebration is in knowing that our God is the source of our strength.

Antithesis:

There are times in life when calamities will cause our life to be unproductive and destroy our witness for the Lord and His church. Though all of satan's weapons are deceptive, the influence of them can destroy families, communities and the church along with its ministries. When these kind of destructive behaviors come our way, they are unproductive. Habakkuk 3:17-19 reminds us that we still have something to celebrate.

SYNTHESIS

Relevant question- How can we celebrate our God?

1. We can celebrate in our God by knowing that God is sovereign. (verse 19)

The same God that has allowed our calamities to take place is the same God that we can turn to for comfort. Our God has everything in control, therefore turning to Him for comfort that this world cannot give is one of the attributes that makes Him sovereign. Like Habakkuk, we too must learn to pray to the sovereign Lord and cast our cares upon Him. God is sovereign in our life and he has the power to change any circumstances that opposes his reign.

2. We can celebrate in our God by knowing that though our lives seem to be unproductive, we can still be joyful in God our Savior. (verse 18) Habakkuk declared that though the fig tree does not bud, no grapes on the vines, though the fields produce no food is a revelation of how sometimes our lives can be unproductive and sometimes our ministries can be unproductive.

3. We can celebrate our God because He gives us strength. (Verse 19) Habakkuk named some things that the people of his day needed in order to be sustained in everyday life. His prayer to God is, I know that our enemy is on their way to destroy us and carry us off into exile, but even if we have nothing left to sustain us, you are still the source of our strength and your strength can enable us to go to heights that we (SJBC) cannot reach on my own.

CONCLUSION:

The declaration that the Lord is my strength: "He makes my feet like the feet of a deer, he enables me to go on the heights", separates us from those who do not trust in God. In our strength in God, we can achieve heights that, otherwise, cannot be obtained. In His strength I can make it. In His strength you can make it. In His strength we will make it. We have something to celebrate.

APPENDIX N 4:   A PERFECT POSTURE FOR THE JOURNEY
LUKE 5:11 – VERSE 5

PROPOSITION:

There are many of us who are gathered here this morning who are serious about our ministries, who also look forward to the fruits of our labor. But often times instead of receiving booming results we find ourselves only surviving, when we compare our gift to the ministries on the other side of town we question what are we doing wrong. Every now and then we must question our methodology of how we do ministry, then ask ourselves what kind of posture is needed to exalt Gods kingdom and promote his agenda effectively.

THESIS:

Our text that is before us reveals how our Lord's early disciples had been practicing their own unproductive methodology of catching fish, but was receptive in allowing Jesus to change their posture for ministry forever. The text reveals that there is no methodology that Jesus cannot perfect. There is always room for improvement in our lives. They were professionals in the natural, but in the supernatural they were amateurs at what Jesus was about to do with them.

ANTITHESIS:

There are times when all of our training, education and experience is not enough to produce the results that God intends for us. We have allowed our years of practice and professionalism to dictate to us that we should have the best results because of our own skills and cognitive ingenuity. We seem to carry that same attitude with us when we become involved in ministry. If we are going to perfect our posture we are going to have to do ministry God's way.

How can we develop the perfect posture for ministry?

SYNTHESIS:

1. There must be a hunger for the word.

The crowd was pressed upon Jesus; they came from near and far with various needs. There is no way that you can have a crowd around Jesus and not have needs "Blessed are ye that hunger now for ye shall be filled". They gathered and crowded around him to hear the word of God.

2. Each of us has something that the Lord can use.

Simon Peter's boat was no different from any other wooden fishing boat of that day, but when the Lord needed it, the anointing in him transformed it into a pulpit. We all have something that we possess that Jesus can use. No gift or talent is too big or too small to give back to him.

3. To have the perfect posture for ministry we must allow our failures to become God's opportunity.

In verse 5, Simon declares Master we have toiled all night and have caught nothing. Nevertheless, at thy word I will let down the net. In order for God to get the glory out of what we do for him, our posture for ministry must be nevertheless...Lord because you say so, I will do it your way. Lord I've been doing things my way but it's been unproductive.

CONCLUSION:

I have been trying to run your auxiliaries my way but it has been unproductive. But nevertheless I need results. Lord because you say so, I am going to drop my net down on the other side and I'm going to wait on you. I can expect your blessings to be so abundant that I will have to share them with others around me. Put the Lord in your ministry and watch him work things out for you. Keep the Lord in your witness and he will draw all unto him.

APPENDIX N 5: WHAT REAL FRIENDS DO

2 KINGS 7:3-9 (9)

PROPOSITION

Friend – One who is attached to another by affection or esteem.

- Acquaintance
- One who is not hostile.
- One that is of the same.
- A favored companion.
- Showing a beneficial or helpful purpose.
- One that promotes harmony and that is not antagonistic.

Friendship – Is more relational and more qualitative then quantitative. It's not about how many friends that I have, but it's about the quality of our relationship. It involves a mutuality of oneness that expands through time in spite of conditions and/or circumstances.

THESIS:

The epitome of that friendship is seen in our text in the history of **2 Kings 7:3-9** during the siege of the city of Samaria by Syria. Four men who were suffering from leprosy sat outside the gate contemplating on how they were going to survive. "….less we die" They began to eat and drank what was there, grabbed the silver, gold, and clothing they found, and went off and hid them; then they returned to another tent and did the same thing. But then they said to each other, we shouldn't be doing this! <u>We have Good News</u>, and we shouldn't keep it to ourselves. Let's go right now and tell the others back home in Samaria.

This is what real friends do! This what real family do! We can't keep this good news to ourselves. For all of the bad news that we have seen and heard in our community and country, **"We've got good news"**

SYNTHESIS:

POINT I

REAL FRIENDS WILL BE SENSITIVE TO EACH OTHERS CONDITION, AND WILL NOT ALLOW THAT TO COME BETWEEN THEM.

The common denominator among them was their condition, and they did not allow that to come between them. Instead they realized that we are all in the same predicament. We are going to stick together like real friends do. You confirm me and I will confirm you. God wants us to become sensitive to the plight of others who are in the same boat as you. Real friends will rejoice with those who rejoice and mourn with those who mourn.

POINT II

WHEN THE ODDS ARE AGAINST YOU, YOU HAVE TO MAKE A DECISION OF FAITH.

They had at least 3 odds stacked against them. 1. They were lepers, 2. They were outcast. 3. It was a bad economy. You got to make a bold decision of faith. Without faith it is impossible to please God. Faith is the substance of things hoped for and the evidence of things not seen. **Hebrews 11:1** He who comes to God must believe that He is, and that He is a rewarder of those who diligently seek Him. **Hebrews 11:6**

POINT III

DON'T BE SELFISH IN YOUR GAIN, BUT BLESS BURDENED PEOPLE

There was an awakening of their sin consciousness. (They said what we are doing is wrong). What we are doing is wrong. Real friends don't do this. This is selfish of us. Thank God that they didn't wear their feelings on their sleeves like some of us do. Instead they said that God has been too good to us. We are outcast living outside of the city gates and there are folk within the city that are dying. Don't allow your condition to keep you from bringing salvation to other people. God can use you to bless burden people. That's what real friends will do! If I can help somebody along the way then my living will not be in vein.

CONCLUSION

1. That's what real friends do.
2. We were just like the lepers....burden down by the care of this world until I heard some Good News. (JESUS) said that I wasn't going to tell nobody, but I couldn't keep it to myself.
3. They had some good news. They didn't want to tell anybody, but if you are going to bless burden people, you've got to share the good news with them.
4. The Good News is Jesus a friend that sticks closer than a brother.

APPENDIX O: SJBC Training Evaluation

Pastor Jerome Lee, Jr., M.DIV

1.   Did the training/conference meet your expectations?

      A. Not met   B. Moderately met   C. Fully met

2.   Did the duration of the training/conference meet your expectations?

      A. Not met   B. Moderately met   C. Fully met

3.   Did the training/conference materials provided meet your expectations?

      A. Not met   B. Moderately met   C. Fully met

4.   Did the facilitator exemplify adequate knowledge of the content?

      A. Not met   B. Moderately met   C. Fully met

5.   Did the facilitator answer questions from the audience to your expectations?

      A. Not met   B. Moderately met   C. Fully met

6.   Did the accessibility of the venue and location of today's training/conference meet your expectations?

      A. Not met   B. Moderately met   C. Fully met

How could this workshop be improved?

_____

_____

_____

_____

Additional Comments:

_____

_____

_____

APPENDIX P: Cumulative Stakeholders Results:

TO DEACON OR NOT TO DEACON

Stakeholders: Deacon, Deaconess, Other/Staff, Minister

The top ten roles/responsibilities stakeholders believed were most important in SJBC deacon ministry ranked in importance.

1. Daily prayer and devotion time

2. Supporting the pastor and the vision God has given him

3. Regular and consistent attendance in Sunday and/or Bible

Study

4. Regular and consistent giving of tithes and offerings

5. Conducting a family care ministry

6. Taking communion to/visiting the healing and recovering

7. Assisting in conducting the ordinances of the church

8. Engaging in outreach to the un-churched (evangelism)

9. Continual spiritual training as a unified diaconate ministry

10. Recognizing and using your spiritual gifts

APPENDIX Q: ST. JAMES BAPTIST CHURCH POTENTIAL

DEACON QUESTIONNAIRE

Name_____ Date_____

DOB_____   Date Joined SJBC_____

This Deacon Questionnaire is a self-assessment tool for Potential Deacon. The questions are designed to allow you to prayerfully and honestly examine yourself in light of Scripture to determine if you meet the Biblical qualifications of Deacon.

1. Do you have a relationship with Jesus Christ as your Lord?

2. Please describe your salvation experience.

3. Do you want to serve as a deacon?

4. Have you served as a deacon before? If so, here_____

5. Do you believe the Bible to be inerrant and infallible Word of God?

6. Have you read the qualifications of a deacon in Acts 6.1-7 and 1st Timothy 3?

7. Are you faithful in your stewardship by tithing to SJBC?

8. Does your spouse support your service as a deacon?

9. Can you be faithful to deacon's meetings primarily on the 2nd Thursday and 3rd Saturday from 9-11am?

10. Are you faithful in your attendance to the Sunday School, Intercessory Prayer, Bible Study?

11. Are you willing to visit members in the hospital and shut-ins?

12. Do you strive to making reading God's Word a daily priority?

13. Will you commit to increasing the amount of time you spend in prayer for the pastor and the church staff and the members?

14. Please explain why you would like to serve as a deacon.

15. In your opinion, what is the mission of the church?

16. Are you willing to abide the church's constitution and bylaws?

17. Are you willing to resign your position as a deacon if you ever reach a point where you could no longer be loyal to the Pastor or support His vision?

I affirm that everything presented in this questionnaire is true and accurate:

Signature: _____

VITA

Jerome Lee, Jr. attended Hampton High School in Hampton Va. He received a Diploma in Christian Ministry from the James P. Boyce College of the Bible of The Southern Baptist Theological Seminary while subsequently working as a crew leader for the City of Hampton Public Works for fifteen years. He received his Master of Divinity in Christian Education in 2005 from The Samuel DeWitt Proctor School of Theology, Virginia Union University. He served as the pastor of the Shiloh Baptist Church, Painter, Virginia for twelve years. Rev. Lee served as the Second Vice- Moderator for the Eastern Shore of Virginia- Maryland Baptist Association and also served as the Association's Director of Christian Education. He currently serves as the pastor of St. James Baptist Church in Greensboro, North Carolina since May 2011. In 2015, he graduated from the Samuel DeWitt Proctor School of Theology, Virginia Union University with the Doctor of Ministry.

Printed in the United States
By Bookmasters